Joyful Adventures is an easy read! I couldn't put it down. I wanted to hear of the next wonderful journey and encounters with God, His healings, His provisions, the supernatural ways Holy Spirit moved in Jeans' life and those around her.

I read with awe and wonder as how Holy Spirit can work in one's life to bring abundant life through an individual who is willing to listen and walk dependently on Him.

There are many keys in this book that will open the way to new adventures for us all if we ask expectantly and we too walk

Sandra Stewart, Leader
"AS ONE North East"

You write well and the end result is a feeling of exhilaration, admiration and thankfulness for all the Lord has done with and through you; and of course Chris' key role as a Kingdom facilitator.
I also found it humbling and sobering to realise again how God continues to use people who are riddled with faults. Wimbur used to say" never trust a man who does not walk with a limp… saying this I am not thinking of you, but sadly some of the people you, I and so many have gained much from who have been showed to have messed up in big ways (such as Bickle and Jones).You have managed to honour the good they gave and point us in your book to the Bigness of God. Thank you.

I see a lot of people getting much encouragement from the book and finding its size easy to get into and pacy to keep you reaching for the next page.

The Reverend, Nigel di Castiglione.
Team Rector, Papworth Team Ministry.

When I think of Jean, I often picture the twinkle in her eye and the warmth of her smile... this book illustrates where that sheer joy for life and love for people comes from: Jean is someone who has said

"Here I am God send me!" , and He has....to people and places all round the world and Jean has discovered how thrilling the journey is when Holy Spirit is leading the way and you see things from His perspective! In the pages you hold in your hands, Jean encourages you to hunger for more of God and believe for fresh encounters with Holy Spirit in your everyday life. Through the stories of her own experiences with Holy Spirit, Jean draws out nuggets of inspiration and truth to spur us on in our own joyful adventures with God.

Helen Azer,
UK Director of Ministry, Heartcry for Change.

I have known Jean since our paths crossed in the Church family which we both made home in 2002. I was transferring from my first force, Greater Manchester Police to West Midlands police at the time so was going through a lot of change. Jean became a faithful friend in those early days. My first vivid recollection was sharing a room with Jean in April 2002 and we both participated in a Prayer assignment in Dover and Greenwich. Jean was as enthusiastic then as she is today! She lives with her cup half full though usually it never gets that low and is always spilling over with loving and serving others wholeheartedly. Her book tells her wonderful story from the time her faith came alive, and details so many incredible adventures she has enjoyed with God since that time. In the mundane as well as the extravagant you will have a chance to meet the big God Jean knows and loves. As you read through the pages you will find yourself experiencing the adventures with Jean, sharing in the same sense of anticipation and excitement about the next instalment as they unfold through each chapter. I have witnessed Jean inspiring and encouraging others as a wonderful role model, wife, mother, grandmother, sister, co-worker and friend. Her story is inspiring and her positivity through these pages is contagious, so get ready to feel motivated and uplifted as you read!

Maria Fox,

Retired Chief Superintendent Derbyshire constabulary,

West Midlands Police and Greater Manchester Police,

Joyful Adventures with God

My Journey with Holy Spirit

Jean Smith

Joyful adventures with God

Paperback ISBN 978-1-0686849-0-6

Editor: Danai Maphosa maphosaedits@gmail.com
Cover design by Jean Smith
Published by Jean Smith
Book interior by C R Smith

Dedication

To my funny, loving, precious grandchildren, Emilia, Oscar, Oliver and Matilda, I love being with you and my prayer is that your lives will be full of amazing adventures.

Acknowledgements

I want to thank my wonderful husband Chris, you have understood little of my God life and yet you are full of His grace. You have been my best supporter ever since the day I met you and have encouraged and released me in my adventures. I love you!

My two wonderful sons, Ben and Tim, you have believed in and encouraged me in the writing in this book from the day I told you about it; I love you.

My heartfelt thanks to Jenny Watson, friend and Apostolic Leader at KAN, who has inspired, encouraged, challenged and been my church leader for the last twenty two years and who mentored me to write this book, you are amazing!

Danai, it was another Holy Spirit conversation that led to you being my Editor. It has been my joy to work with you and I thank God for you.

Ashley! I was asked to help you write a book but you have helped me far more, thank you dear friend for your texts, the "gram" and publishing help....

My brother Peter who spent part of his sailing holiday with us, re-arranging my manuscript files!

Suzanne without you this might not have happened when I lost all the work on my computer and you found it!

Adeline, thank you for the great photo!

To my crazy, "odd" and lovely friends at KAN, I thank God for every one of you and for your wonderful encouragement; I am amazed how He has brought us all together for His Kingdom purposes. And there is so much more!

Contents

Forward

You are unlikely to meet anyone as passionate, genuine and capable of making others smile as the author- who luckily for me, happens to be my Mum. Her infectious personality shines through every page. I loved reading about the journey Mum's had and is continuing to have.

A book about faith, family and friendship; something that all of us can relate to in some way.

Tim Smith
Son, Father, Company Director
Orderley London

Forward

God has set inside each one of us *longings of the human heart* imparted that we may search for and find the satisfaction and fulfillment for our lives.

Those longings enable us to scale barriers, push through limitations and achieve incredible milestones. This book is a catalogue of memoirs, weaving the story of one who searched, found and on her own journey discovered much about herself, life, eternity and the God she now loves and serves, by way of fantastic adventures.

I have had the privilege of knowing Jean Smith for over 22 years; we have journeyed, laughed, cried, made discoveries, and travelled together. I count her as one of my closest friends, dependable, honest, transparent, and passionate and always holding the *glass half full* rather than *glass half empty*

perspective on life situations! This makes her a wonderful example of faith and hope in the KAN ministry community that we belong to.

The book you hold in your hand is a truthful account of Jean's personal God encounters and exploits; it delivers what it promises by the title.

However if you will take time to allow these accounts to settle on your heart, you will find woven between the lines, divine invitations and teachings that will promote faith, spark off questions and truly inspire you to reach out and trust in this awesome God that Jean calls Father, Jesus the one and only Savior and Holy Spirit who was sent into the world to complete the plan of the Godhead; salvation for all mankind.

There are many self-help books on the shelves, readily available, but few carry the authentic reality of feet- on- the- ground accounts of the ordinary becoming extra-ordinary or the natural becoming super- natural in the day to day hum drum of life. It is also worth noting that this documentary spans many years and Jean has delightfully incorporated periods of true growth and maturity. I believe that Holy Spirit has found a resting place in Jeans heart due to simple obedience and incredible willingness to allow Him to adjust her time after time. I don't know of many who have this capacity and quality to refuse to be offended and to readily accept a course correction or adjustment. I have seen , and you can read for yourself, how Jean has taken leaps of faith that have paid off in answered prayers, and divine accomplishments- this is the true reward of obediently serving Jesus. I commend this book and my lovely friend Jean Smith to you dear reader. You are in for a great ride, and potentially your own God encounter as you open your heart and dive in!

My prayer is that seeds of faith and joy will be sown in you. Enjoy!

Jenny Watson
Coach, Author, Apostolic Leader
Kingdom Advance Network

Cover

A dear friend said to me 'Holy Spirit says,

"It is time to put up the spinnaker."

The Spinnaker is a balloon shaped sail, often brightly coloured and made of very light nylon, used for sailing with the direction of the wind.

There is nothing quite like raising the spinnaker and watching as the wind fills it from behind and the feeling of exhilaration as the boat moves through the water.

As long as the boat is moving in the direction of the wind even the lightest wind will have a dramatic effect!

" the wind blows where it wishes and you hear the sound of it, but do not know where it comes from and where it is going; so is everyone who is born of the spirit"

John 3:8 NASB

James Goll in his book" The Seer" says,

"This is a word for every believer; all of us who are born again are to catch the wind of the spirit. There are some people; however who seem to have an anointing to catch that wind more than others. They wet their finger, stick it up in the air to find out which way the wind is blowing, then set their sails and follow that wind wherever it goes."

In 2015 we bought our first sailing boat and when my husband Chris surprisingly asked me to suggest names for the boat we agreed to call it "An Geadh Glas," or "Wild Goose," which is the Celtic name for Holy Spirit.

Mark Batterson on the cover of his book "the Wild Goose Chase" says,

"The name hints at mystery, much like a wild goose, the spirit of God cannot be tracked or tamed. An element of danger, an air of unpredictability surrounds Him. And while the name might sound a little sacrilegious, I cannot think of a better description of what it is like to follow the spirit through life. I think the Celtic Christians were on to something.......most of us will have no idea where we are going most of the time and I know that is unsettling. But circumstantial uncertainty also goes by another name...

Adventure."

Although Holy Spirit is usually depicted as a dove, with His reputation for gentleness and calmness, An Geadh Glas seemed an appropriate name to call our boat.

Life following Holy Spirit is an adventure and we did not have any idea where Holy Spirit was going to take us. Spanning decades and continents, this book chronicles some of my amazing adventures with Holy Spirit.

Introduction

"Jean, there is a vault inside of you, a vault of many books that you have not yet written. Tonight I am turning the combination and opening it up inside of you."

(Prophecy, Santa Rosa Beach 2007)

God is going to use you to stir up other workers, you are going to equip them, you are going to empower them and they are going to talk about things that you write and things that you say. Do not play small, it does not glorify God. Unless you play to the full stature of whom you He created you to be.

You have been productive, so you are going to have to release some of the things that you have hidden, that no one even knows that you have got, and it is going to be hard for you because you do not want to promote yourself. But ultimately you are really promoting God because He is the one who gave it to you. He is your coach and he is the one who put it in your heart, so do not worry about what other people say, and do not worry about the criticism or fear of failure. God is with you and it is going to be a lot of fun, a lot of things will be really special for you that will be meaningful for you, you will know that they are from the Lord.

Go and tell other people about it and let them have fun too!!
Prophecy, Burton 2009

"The Lord is raising you up as a woman who is pleased to be a woman, to minister to women who are struggling in this area with hurts and needs, so that they can in turn help others .You will be able to minister out of the word of God to people who are struggling in the whole area of womanhood. It is empowering women to be mighty, it is saying you are a mighty woman of God , this is how you do it and this is how you operate as a woman of God in domesticity , in the workplace, ministry etc. restoring equal ruler ship like the original design for Adam and Eve."
Prophecy, 2004.

For the last 25 years I have written a Journal/ Diary of teachings and experiences as I have lived as a Christian believer. I believe that God speaks to His people.

"The sheep that are my own hear and are listening to my voice; and I know them and they follow me. "
John 10:27 Amplified Bible

I had discovered early in the '90's in my local Anglican church that our God is a personal God and wants a relationship with us, and all relationships need communication. God is not a remote God, He is looking for friends.

*"And so the scripture was fulfilled that says, Abraham believed in adhered to, trusted in, and relied on God, and this was accounted to him as righteousness (as conformity to God's will in thought and deed) and he was called **God's friend.**"*

James 2:23 Amplified bible

David who knew God as his best friend said,

"How precious also, are Your thoughts to me, O God! How great is the sum of them. If I should count them they would be more in number than the sand; when I awake, I am still with you."

Psalm 139:17-18

God spoke to Adam and Eve,

"And they heard the sound of the Lord God walking in the garden........................then Lord called to Adam and said to him 'where are you?' I heard your voice in the garden and I was afraid because I was naked; and I hid myself."

Genesis 3:8-10

The entire Bible is full of God speaking to His people. God's desire and design is to have free flowing communication with mankind. Ever since the Garden man's sin has dulled man's ability to hear His voice, He has chosen other means of communication.

He found messengers, the prophets, who would speak His message to the people.

God sent His son Jesus to talk to us about our heavenly father.

God uses the written word, the Bible to reveal to us the mind, the will and the purposes of God.

God sent His Holy Spirit to be the vehicle that He would talk to us through.

God spoke to Peter and to the Apostle Paul in Acts in the New Testament and to John in the book of Revelation and to many people throughout the Bible and He has not stopped speaking to us. I am amazed that the God who created the heavens and the earth wants to have a friendship with me and you.

This book is full of stories, encounters, prophecies and experiences from nearly forty years of Journaling and every word has reminded me that we have an amazing, wonderful loving heavenly Father.

"Lord you know everything there is to know about me".
You perceive every movement of my heart and soul, and you understand my every thought before it even enters my mind. You are so intimately aware of me, Lord.

You read my heart like an open book and you know all the words I am about to speak before I even start a sentence! You know every step I will take before my journey even begins."

Psalm 139:1-4 TPT.

Thank you Holy Spirit for this journey together!

Chapter 1

My History is His Story Through Me

"... (You came to know the grace or undeserved favour of God in reality, deeply and clearly and thoroughly and becoming accurately and intimately acquainted with it.)"
Colossians 1:6 (Amplified Bible, Classic Edition)

Life changed in May 1984 when belief turned into reality.

My upbringing in a Christian family and going to church had taught me that Jesus loved me but on that amazing day, faith came into play and reality hit me. I NOW KNEW THAT JESUS LOVED *ME*!

The great Evangelist, Billy Graham, had come to do a Mission in England and the church was hosting gatherings in football stadiums all over the country. The atmosphere was electric when we arrived as the choir was singing the worship song, Majesty.

"Majesty, worship his majesty, unto Jesus, be all glory and honour and praise.

Majesty, Kingdom authority, flow from his throne, unto his own, his anthem raise.

So exalt, lift up on high, the name of Jesus, magnify, come glorify, Christ Jesus, the King.

Majesty, worship his majesty, Jesus who died, now glorified, King of all Kings."

Even as a long standing football supporter, I had never heard such singing.

The stadium was full with 50,000 people who were chattering excitedly. I was part of a team praying for and taking people to the event, but God hijacked me! At some point I heard Billy Graham say, "Jesus loves you" and he could have easily added, "Jean Smith" because I knew that he was speaking directly to me. God was calling me by name.

"Everything we could ever need for life and complete devotion to God has already been deposited in us by his divine power. For all this was lavished upon us through the rich experience of knowing him who has ***called us by name*** *and invited us to come to him through a glorious manifestation of his goodness."*

2 Peter 1:3 TPT.

I had never felt such love sweep over and through me; I knew in that instant that Jesus was real. Of all the people that I took to that event it was me that gave my life to Jesus that day! I said yes to follow Jesus and I was born again.

*"Jesus said to him (*Nicodemus*), 'Most assuredly I say to you, unless one is born again, he cannot see the kingdom of God.' Nicodemus said to Him, 'How can a man be born when he is old? Can he enter a second time into his mother's womb and be born? Who is born of the spirit?'"*

"Jesus answered 'Most assuredly I say to you, unless one is born of water and the Spirit, he cannot enter the Kingdom of God. That which is born of the flesh is flesh, and that which is born of the Spirit is spirit. Do not marvel that I said to you, you must be born again. The wind blows where it wishes, and you hear the sound of it, but cannot tell where it comes from and where it goes. So is everyone who is born of the spirit.'"

John 3:3-8

One of the first signs that life for me had changed was that the Bible came to life!

Holy Spirit began to challenge me about what the Bible really said, I found myself checking what the Vicar was preaching and teaching: I vividly remember the story of the loaves and fishes being taught and we were told "the boy shared his food and as a result everyone else shared their food," as soon as I got home I was searching for the story.

"'Gather up the fragments that remain, so that nothing is lost.' Therefore they gathered them up, and filled twelve baskets with the fragments of the five barley loaves which were left over by those who had eaten. Then those men, when they had seen the sign that Jesus did, said, 'This is truly the Prophet who is to come into the world.'"

John 6:12-14

From that day in the stadium, the words of the Bible came to life and so began a joyful adventure with a big God.

At the time I was attending my local Anglican church, and with my friend Sue, occasionally visiting a larger and livelier church on a Sunday evening to get topped up. One Sunday evening we were driving through our local town and heard the church bells ringing, we sensed that we were to go there. It was a very normal evensong but as we left the Vicar invited us to a midweek gathering in the crypt and teaching on the gifts of the

Holy Spirit and he promised us that it would be a little more exciting than the service we had had!! We were hooked and Tuesday night did not fail to draw us further in. So began our adventure at St Edithas', Tamworth, led by Vicar John Widdas. He with his Curate Peter, introduced us to Holy Spirit, and the gifts of the Spirit, which he taught on and then activated us to use every week in the crypt of the church.

"Each believer is given continuous revelation by the Holy Spirit to benefit not just Himself but all. For example:
The Spirit gives to one a message of wisdom,
To another the same Spirit gives the gift of the word of revelation knowledge.
And to another, the same Spirit gives the gift of faith.
And to another the same Spirit gives gifts of healing.
And to another the power to work miracles.
And to another the gift of prophecy.
And to another the gift to discern what the Spirit is speaking.
And to another the gift of speaking different kinds of tongues.
And to another the interpretation of tongues.
1 Corinthians 12:7-11.TPT.

What fun we had, we were like children in a sweet shop.

These were also the days of "March for Jesus", On September 15, 1990 more than 200,000 marched for Jesus in 600 cities all over Britain, and we marched through Tamworth with many other churches, singing songs written specially for these events by

Graham Kendrick, songs such as "Shine Jesus Shine" and "I Will Build My Church".

These were exciting years, at the same time I was bringing up my two wonderful sons, Ben and Tim, and trying to get some time off to follow wherever Holy Spirit was leading. In these years, my friend Sue and I went to hear John Wimber, the Kansas City Prophets and many others. We were hungry for all that Holy Spirit could feed us with.

Chapter 2

Time to Get Ready

I had started to visit a convent in Derby on retreat, spending time with the delightful anointed Sister Pippa, who was a gift from God to me. Lunch was eaten in the dining room, in silence, which for a chatterbox like me proved to be a challenge. Silence did, however, prove to be golden. As I ate, a vision unfolded of a young horse that was being broken in and led around the training ring by a handler; it was trying to get away and do its own thing. I was aware that in order to be of use it needed training. I was that horse. My money, my house, and my future were to become the training ground for a life being led by Holy Spirit.

In 1994 the tangible presence of God settled on a church near Toronto Airport in Canada. Many from the UK went out to experience and see for themselves how Holy Spirit was moving and brought *"it"* back! The British press called *"it"* the Toronto Blessing.

I went to one of a few hubs in the UK that had experienced this blessing, St Andrews Chorleywood, Hertfordshire, I found that I could easily relate to this and wanted this experience for myself.

Fast forward to August -

Each year several churches would join together for a summer festival called New Wine, a festival that gathers Christians from all over the country. Annie and Nigel were instrumental in getting us there! Nigel, the new Curate, of my local Anglican church and his wife and family were thirsty for more of God. We all went and it was to become a yearly, much needed spiritual visit for my friend Sue and I taking a selection of tents, a caravan and one year a motorhome to the week-long conference.

One of my favourite speakers was James Ryle from the USA. His definition of Grace, which I love, is "the empowering presence of God enabling me to be all that he created me to be and to do all that he had created me to do" but he also challenged me in his many talks about tithing, giving 10% of my income to the service of God. This was new teaching to me as I had been raised as an Anglican and had never heard about tithing. I was a stay at home Mum with no income and my husband, Chris, had not yet encountered Jesus. As you can imagine me giving money to the church was a touchy subject!

"You have sown much, and bring in little; You eat, but do not have enough; You drink, but you are not filled with drink; You clothe yourselves, but no one is warm; And he who earns wages, earns wages to put into a bag with holes.
Thus says the Lord of hosts:
'Consider your ways! .... You looked for much, but indeed it came to little; and when you brought it home, I blew it away.
Why?'
Says the Lord of hosts.
'Because of My house that is in ruins, while every one of you runs to his own house. Therefore the heavens above you withhold the dew, and the earth withholds its fruit.'"

Haggai 1:6-10

I did not know how the Lord was going to make tithing possible but I was in for a surprise!

Chris's job as head of engineering was very demanding and he was commuting 70 miles each way just to get to his office as well as long distances to visit work sites. One day Chris surprised me by arriving home in the middle of the day with the news that he no longer had a job; he had been made redundant! The company were restructuring as the market was changing and they no longer needed his expertise, so were shutting his department down.

To say this was a shock was an understatement: we had no income and we had school fees to pay! I found myself saying out loud "this will be a blessing in disguise," which he was not ready to hear.

Within three months, he was echoing these very words!

This happened in 1999, shortly after praying a prayer to which the answer was heralded by this pivotal moment. Nigel, now my Vicar and my very wise friend suggested I walk the boundary of our house and submit it to God. I later learned that this was a prayer of consecration. Although we loved living in our very special old house, which we had completely renovated, it was too far away from work, so a decision to move had to be made. That prayer of consecration was a response to that need. Jesus submitted His will to His Father's and I was trusting God with my family home! The redundancy was a catalyst to the answer to more than one prayer.

Part of Chris's leaving package was the ability to take early retirement at 50, which was 3 months away. We decided to go for that option, which would provide a safety net (a small pension) as he had decided to start his own company as a consultant to take advantage of the changing market. To facilitate that, I was on the payroll, with a separate income and as a result was able to tithe my earnings!

My prayer had been answered, not as I expected but I learned that my Heavenly Father can be trusted to know what is best for me.

I was later to read in the amazing book "The Merismos" about the breaking and training of a young horse that what is really broken in the horse is the strength of its will; if it is trained it does not have to be broken!

"a trained horse will respond to a gentle tug having developed sensitivity, we are to be the meek, the sensitive of spirit, those who have come under submission and control of Holy Spirit because of being dealt with in the soulish realm, that when God makes a turn, you almost instantly respond to His gentle tug on the reins of your heart."

The Merismos

"The sacrifices of God are a broken spirit, a broken and contrite heart. These, O God, You will not despise."

Psalm 51:17

The meaning for *broken* in Strong's Bible Concordance #7665 is the Hebrew word *shabar:* to burst, break, bring to birth. The root word for *heart* in Hebrew refers *to inner man or will.* To have a broken heart means that we are willing to put off our natural man and yield our will to God's will.

In the breaking there can be new birth!

"My children don't underestimate the value of the discipline and training of the Lord God, or get depressed when He has to correct you. For the Lord's training of your life is the evidence of His unfailing love"

Hebrews 12:5-6 TPT.

In being challenged to yield my money, my house, and my future into my Heavenly Father's hands, I believe the question I was being asked by Holy Spirit was, "Are you willing to trust me with your life?"

Chapter 3

Here I am Lord, Send Me

"'Go therefore and make disciples of all the nations, baptising them in the name of the Father and of the Son and the Holy Spirit, teaching them to observe all things that I have commanded you; and lo, I am with you always, even to the end of the age. Amen."

Matthew 28:19-20

Opportunities to go and spread the gospel don't come around often and when they do, we are not always daring enough to take them.

My niece Rachel has a favourite saying: "shy bairns get nowt," meaning ASK! I had been reading an article in a magazine about overseas Missions training with a church in Exeter and thought: "why not write to them and ask if you can go to be trained?"

Having no prior association with them, I decided to follow through with this thought and wrote to them. To my astonishment, they replied and said yes! But it was a three week trip. Since getting married, I had never spent three weeks away from home without Chris, so it was no small thing to consider. I pondered over what Chris would think. What would he say?

Three weeks!

When I wrote to them, I was actually expecting to be attending a course about missions in Exeter and this quickly evolved into an invitation to India. I had not met any of the party before and they did not know me, but Holy Spirit did!

One thing was clear; no progress was to be made simply thinking about it. I thought the Lord was in this but I needed to pray! Prayer is not manipulation that would be witchcraft! Prayer is simply talking to God and developing a personal relationship with Him.

As we get to know Him and sense His ways, we come into agreement with His ways and thoughts. I was expecting reservations and questions and the need for persuasion, but Chris was very encouraging and immediately said "you must go, this is a great opportunity" to say I was astonished was an understatement!

But that year, 1999, he had travelled to Rio de Janeiro for work. His experience was so marvellous that he was excited for me. It turned out to be a year of acceleration for both of us. Different countries at different times amounted to a shared experience of adventure. A few weeks later, he drove me to Heathrow with my guitar to meet my three fellow travellers and fly to India: home for the next three weeks.

My initial first memories and sights of Delhi were potholed roads, incredible traffic, auto rickshaws, cars, trucks, cows, camels, elephants and people all weaving in and out, vying for position. There was the constant noise of horns, dogs and cockerels, as well as the smells of diesel, exhausts and food, which was an overwhelming feast for my senses.

How did I get here? By simply asking!

This Scripture would prove to be a key in my walk with Holy Spirit, Matthew 7:7-11

"Ask, and it will be given to you; seek, and you will find; knock, and it will be opened to you. For everyone who asks receives, and he who seeks finds, and to him who knocks it will be opened. Or what man is there among who, if his son asks for bread, will give him a stone? Or if he asks for a fish, will he give him a serpent? If you then, being evil, know how to give good gifts to your children, how much more will your Father who is in heaven give good things to those who ask Him!"

Amazingly, God always gives us more than we can ask or expect! At the time, I had no idea that my trip to India would lead to church family where I am now, several trips to the USA and even more adventures in God.

"Never doubt God's mighty power to work in you and accomplish all this. He will achieve infinitely more than your greatest request, your most unbelievable dream, and exceed your wildest imagination! He will outdo them all, for his miraculous power constantly energises you."

Ephesians 3:20 TPT

We arrived in Delhi and met the rest of our small team, a family from Portland Oregon, and a mother and son from Israel. What an amazing team the Lord had put together! The nine of us very quickly learnt to work together with massive help from and by the power of Holy Spirit. It had to be supernatural! I believe we were all equipped by Him with such grace for each other: Stuart, Cynthia and their daughter Sesha, from America, were to become valued friends and became one of two key connections for me.

As we gathered to worship for the first time together, the doubts crept in: "Why are you here? Who do you think you are?" But also, I heard Holy Spirit saying, "I have anointed you to come and give my anointed Word". I was reminded of the story of Ruth in the Bible; as she gleaned beyond her borders, trusting in God, He gave her a rich harvest – certainly more than she had expected!

Our first visit was to minister at the Nagaland Student church, a lovely Bamboo structure at the University of Delhi. Every student we prayed for was either studying Law or Medicine and they were eager, hungry, young people with such open hearts for Jesus. They had nothing but yet they had everything.

I met Pastors who welcomed us and gave us such freedom to minister to their precious flock. To many, such as Nina and Conrad, we were the encouragement they needed to press on through the difficulties and spiritual warfare they were experiencing. They were renewed Catholics who, for two years, had led the Pentecostal church of the Good Shepherd in Prayagraj, formerly Allahabad. The Lord always does more than we think because I did not know that meeting Conrad was to be a major stepping stone for God's plan for my life.

Prayagraj is the headquarters of all the Indian political parties. A place where the religious and political spirits meet. They were right in the middle of a spiritual stronghold, positioned on the confluence of the three major Hindu holy rivers: the Ganges, the Yamuna and Saraswati rivers.

Millions of Hindus flock to these rivers, offering to the holy men and their gods and walking in the filthy waters where funeral ashes are scattered and even dead bodies! Conrad and Nina

Menzies have an amazing life-giving ministry dedicated to these folk and we were there to encourage them, hold up their arms, stand with them, always reminding them that Jesus won the victory on the cross and defeated the enemy.

"For we do not wrestle against flesh and blood, but against principalities, against powers, against the rulers of the darkness of this age, against spiritual hosts of wickedness in the heavenly places."

Ephesians 6:12

They were hosting a worship conference, and we were in the worship team despite the fact that we had never played together and I could only play three chords! The important thing was we were willing. It so reminds me of the late Vineyard church leader John Wimber's favourite four lettered prayer: HELP– It's the prayer of faith. We so often back off, but Holy Spirit is ready and waiting for our cry of help and really everyone there just wanted more of Jesus.

Each evening there we prayed for hours with hungry and desperate people. There were girls who were under pressure from their families to marry and many who were married, living in abusive relationships. It was such a privilege to pray with them, having heard the cry of their hearts, sharing their pain and leaving them encouraged and strengthened in the Lord.

From there, we boarded the second-class air-conditioned train up to the North, the air conditioning in the toilet was provided by a hole in the floor of the train. It proved to be quite a challenge to balance whilst relieving ourselves! The smell permeating our carriage was of mothballs, which was an attempt to keep the cockroaches away. They must have worked as we did not see any! Or was it prayer? Nevertheless, we had much joy on the journey!

Our next base was Nainital, a lovely town in the foothills of the Himalayas.

It was so cold that we wore everything we had at the same time and slept with our heads facing a three-bar electric fire trying to keep warm. Pastor George and Joyce Irwin and their two sons were our wonderful, loving hosts

Once again it was a joy to meet, pray with and encourage the locals and their precious leaders.

Our prayer times were full of Holy Spirit whisperings. These included thoughts and pictures which when brought together gave us the prophetic word, vision and a plan for our next gathering. As you can imagine our times together were always exciting, challenging and faith building. Holy Spirit is the best intercessor (one who prays or stands in between to bring together.)

"That is what I meant when I said that He (the Spirit) will take the things that are Mine and will reveal (declare, disclose, transmit) it to you".

John 16:15 AMPC.

The Passion Translation says,

"...the Divine Encourager will receive what is Mine and reveal it to you."

I love that picture of Holy Spirit as part of the Godhead bringing to us what Jesus is hearing from the Father! And we have the privilege to tune into that conversation, wow! Holy Spirit is constantly working on our behalf.

Our next place to minister was Dehradun. The journey by bus up to Dehradun (centre of the Basmati rice production) at 700m high took all day. Leaving at 9pm, travelling through the night and arriving at 5pm, it was eye opening as we passed through many villages. Dung mounds by the side of the road, carefully formed in three tiers to be sold as fuel–they did look very attractive! There was field upon field of sugarcane being threshed outside straw roofed houses. This part of India is very flat, the journey in theory should not have taken long as the roads were straight but oxcarts, bicycles, and wandering cows were everywhere, especially where we wanted to go!

We drove through a teak farm and the Rajaji National Park with monkeys on the side of the road. It was beautiful, especially as we began to climb into the foothills, although much drier and dustier than I thought it would be. Eventually we arrived at the Retreat Centre, where the Conference was to be held. We were dirty, hungry and tired. My initial reaction was one of disappointment as there was no one to greet us or offer us a refreshing cup of tea, as we were the first to arrive, but these really were first world problems! Also, Holy Spirit reminded me of the words on a card given to me as I left from one of my house group members.

"The Lord is the one who goes ahead of you. He will be with you; He will not desert you or abandon you, do not fear or be dismayed."

Deuteronomy 31:8 NASB

We, the ladies were sharing a room with a shower or should I say a tap and a jug and a squatty toilet, excellent for our leg muscles! We were fed and had a good sleep.

The following morning, we were praying and the Lord gave one of the team a revelation something the Lord wanted to communicate. The image or picture was of a silk purse with us all sitting inside it. It had a drawstring top, and we were being pulled together in the palm of our heavenly Father's loving, caring and gentle hands. We were offering up our praise and worship which was being funnelled up to heaven through the top of the purse. We felt protected and held. This place was to be an oasis: a safe and loving place for all who were due to attend. We sensed that the Lord was asking us to rest in Him and yield to Him to shape our lives over the next three days. Many who came were missionaries working in Tibet, which was just over the border; they needed a place of rest–an oasis!

My overriding memory of the time in India was of our very powerful prayer times, one of them in Mussoorie, a Himalayan hill station where we prayed together with an American couple who led prayer training for Youth with a Mission, (YWAM). It was my first experience of a heavy anointing (in other words supernatural power to pray. Holy Spirit set us on fire that day in a little room in the mountains that was to affect the rest of my life.

We couldn't leave India without going shopping in a motorised Rickshaw, the drivers were eager to take us to the fancy emporiums for the tourists full of knickknacks but we had heard about Fab India, where we could buy Western style clothes made with Indian fabrics, and it did not disappoint. Several hours later we emerged very happy with our bags full of bargains.

On our last evening in India, we were reunited with the wonderful students at the Nagaland Student Church. At the end of the service, every student asked us to pray for them to be empowered by Holy Spirit for the work they were to do for the

Lord and their Pastor said "everything we asked God for, we got."

At the end of a life changing time in India, the students took us back to the YWCA (where we were staying) by squeezing twelve of us in a Land Rover, which normally would seat 6!

Our goodbyes at Delhi airport were very tearful; the Lord had knit us together as a family. My lasting memory for our parting was from Stuart, Cynthia and Sesha, "come and see us if you are ever in Portland USA."

I had no idea what prophetic words they were for my future, how Holy Spirit would use a series of events over the next few years to get Chris and I to the USA and Portland, enabling me to spend more time with this precious family.

Chapter 4

New Beginnings

"And He has made from one blood every nation of men to dwell on all the face of the earth, and has determined their pre-appointed times and the boundaries of their dwellings."

Acts 17:26

Things were changing for me, I was about to move, not a geographic house relocation but to a new Church family.

Conrad the Pentecostal church leader from Prayagraj, formerly Allahabad, was coming to London to speak at **Prayer for the Nations** and I went to hear him. It was there that I was astonished to hear about a prayer school opening in Burton-on-Trent, which was only 10 miles away from where I lived.

I joined the Prayer School, run and hosted by Stephen (Steve) and Jenny Watson, as it launched in May 2001. I discovered they were "my tribe"- it was just a perfect fit and shortly after I joined Kingdom Advance Network (KAN) the church they lead. (Though at that time the Ministry was operating under a different name)

Prior to joining KAN, I had a conversation with my husband which ended up with a painful decision. I had always been an Anglican and had even started exploring the route to ordination. In my mind at the time, it seemed to me that ordination was the only way to serve Jesus more fully. In hindsight the role of Vicar would have stifled and limited me. Holy Spirit was shaping me to be a "square peg to fit a square hole" – He always knows best, and so did Chris: something I've learnt over many years of marriage is that often, surprisingly, God speaks very clearly through my husband!

I vividly remember the conversation in the car with Chris which ended with that decision: training for me to be ordained was never going to work with family life! Our youngest son, Tim, was still at school and we had all become very used to me holding the fort at home.

It was after moving to my new church in Burton-on-Trent that I remembered this conversation and realised that it had taken place just along the road from where KAN is located, in other words where one journey ended another began. I was continuing my journey of being a God chaser and He was leading me on the right path!

Looking back on what seemed like a massive loss was in fact an amazing gain.

"For I Am knows the thoughts, plans and intentions that I Am thinking toward you, says the Lord, thoughts of peace and not of evil, to give you a future and a hope."
Jeremiah 29:11 (One New Man Bible)

Chris has said many times that KAN is perfect for me as he sees me thrive in the constant changing pattern of life there, and today as I remember where I was 21 years ago and see where I am now, it really is a perfect fit!! I am no longer a square peg in a round hole.

I asked Jenny to share with me why they established KAN and she said,

We had already decided and believed that the Lord wanted us to move back to Burton. We knew that the Lord was calling us back to start a work, which I only knew to be a church.

However, a prophet who we met asked about this: the challenge was, "If the Lord is moving you back to a place where there are Spirit filled churches, then it will be with a particular distinction or intention. Have you any idea what that particular distinction is?"

Out of my mouth came the words, "Yes I know that it's the power and demonstration of the Holy Spirit." I then realised that was a scripture,

"And my speech and preaching was not with enticing words of man's wisdom, but in demonstration of the Spirit and of power."

1 Corinthians 4:4

The Passion translation says,

"The message I preached and how I preached it was not an attempt to sway you with persuasive arguments but to prove to you the almighty power of God's Holy Spirit. For God intended that your faith not be established on man's wisdom but by trusting in his almighty power."

This was another ah-ha moment because if my life has been following and having adventures with Holy Spirit, then KAN was the perfect church for me!

Prayer school was so exciting! Each week we met on Tuesday night and all day Wednesday. It was a mixture of the prophetic (hearing Gods voice leading us together) and spiritual warfare best explained by assertive and authoritative prayer focused on land, regions and Nations as well as personal needs, and Israel focused teaching and prayer. Our prayer times were and still are, exciting, fun and targeted; we always tried as we learned during those formative years to trust the Holy Spirit to lead us. I still liken it to a jigsaw puzzle where each one of us gets a piece of a puzzle and together we see the whole picture. I am still amazed at how Holy Spirit continually speaks to us and encourages us.

The Lord has put together and fashioned an incredible team of people who make room for each other to express their God-given spiritual gifts and who know their God and enjoy doing exploits together.

"But the people who know their God shall be strong and carry out great exploits"

Daniel 11:32

From an early age I thought that the grass was greener on the other side! I had been the first in my family to leave home to go to college. I knew that there was a big world out there and I wanted to see it! Being part of KAN gave me more opportunities to see and experience new adventures. I believe that we miss so much of what God wants to show us because we miss the nudging of Holy Spirit: He is our Creator, He is our Father, He wants to share His creation with us. Even as I write this today God is showing me that He is the God of "more than" and beckoning me to dream big.

"Never doubt God's mighty power to work in you and accomplish all this. He will achieve infinitely more than your greatest request, your most unbelievable dream, and exceed your wildest imagination! He will outdo them all, for His miraculous power constantly energises you."

Ephesians 3:20 (TPT)

I love this Scripture! Our God is big, our God is close to us, and our God has plans for us, big adventures for us, because Jesus died to bring life in its fullness.

"I have come to give you everything in abundance, more than you expect, life in its fullness until you overflow."

John 10:10 (TPT)

How many of us are truly living that life?

Looking back between 2000 and 2006 I had Holy Spirit accelerated training, which included visits to **Christian International Ministries** (CIM) led by Bishop Hamon in Santa Rosa Beach, Florida where we experienced spiritual warfare training at an increased level. This was led by the wonderful Martha Lucia (who has since gone to be with the Lord). She was the "General" of intercession and had a prayer room that looked like a war room where her prayer troops met. We were privileged to be trained and taught by her when she spent almost a year in the UK based with us in Burton-on-Trent.

In her book "Rules of Engagement" Martha writes,

> **"Each time we seek to advance the Kingdom of God on earth we encounter opposing forces of darkness. This means war, because the enemy does not want to relinquish any of his territory or persons he holds in bondage, and he will fight against anyone who seeks to unseat him from his realms of control. Therefore we must become skilled warriors...as we seek to know God experientially; He will reveal His truth to us and help us to accomplish His purposes."**

The Passion translation says it like this,

"God's high and holy praises fill their mouths, for their shouted praises are their weapon of war! These warring weapons will bring vengeance on every opposing force and every resisting power to bind kings with chains and rulers with iron shackles. Praise filled warriors will enforce the judgement doom decreed against their enemies. This is the glorious honour He gives to all His godly lovers. Hallelujah Praise the Lord!"

Psalm 149:6-9

and

"Finally, my brethren, be strong in the Lord and in the power of His might. Put on the whole armour of God, that you may be able to stand against the wiles of the devil. For we do not wrestle against flesh and blood, but against principalities, against powers, against the rulers of the darkness of this age, against spiritual hosts of wickedness in the heavenly places. Therefore take up the whole armour of God that you may be able to withstand in the evil day, and having done all, to stand."

Ephesians 6:10-13

Most of the church even today have no clue that if we are commanded to put on the full armour of God, then that means that we are going to be soldiers for Christ as the old hymn goes "Onward Christian soldiers marching as to war with the cross of Jesus going on before!"

"You've trained me with weapons of warfare worship..."

Psalm 18:34 (TPT)

The Christian International Ministry Centre also equipped us in prophecy (how to hear Gods voice and learn how to convey that to others in a relevant and meaningful way, this was a powerful place to visit and personally receive up to date powerful prophetic words)

Combined with Christian International's anointed authority to teach and train in Prophecy, this was a powerful place to be as many prophetic words came out of those visits.

One of my early trips to CIM was as part of a team of four, with my lovely friend Jean we were known as the "pair of Jeans" from the house of LEVI!-the Levites were one of the twelve tribes of Israel-this became a longstanding joke amongst our team. I had been asked to share a room with her and probably felt that I was there to make up numbers.

But as I arrived, someone came up to me with a Word from the Holy Spirit,

"You are not here to make up numbers, but it is a personal invitation from your heavenly Father."

Wow! I just had to receive the invite! There is always joy on the journey, and what an immense joy and privilege it was to go on those trips and many more.

My first prayer assignment to Rome with the CIM team was in September of 2003. It was to be followed by many more since to Naples, Berlin and Brussels. Subsequently, I asked the Lord a question: why do we do these prayer journeys?

"Your feet shod with righteousness have walked these streets for me, Jean, you have been salt and light and you have spread my hope, my joy, and my destiny for the people of Rome. You have been my ambassador, my royal emissary, just as royalty leave an impact and their visit is looked forward to, talked about and remembered so it is for you. You Jean, my daughter, have visited Rome on behalf of me, your Lord, your Redeemer and your King."

We do not have a full understanding of how the spiritual realm works and how our obedience to be in the right place at the right time breaks through for the Kingdom of God. But I often imagine the many possible ah ha moments when I arrive in heaven and see what we have all done to advance God's Kingdom!

One day at Prayer School in Burton in November 2004 as we prayed for the election due to take place in the USA, the Lord spoke to me about Chris working in the USA.

"I will give you the treasures of darkness and hidden riches of secret places, that you may know that I, the Lord, who call you by your name, Am the God of Israel."

Isaiah 45:3

At the time Chris was exploring working in the United States and I sensed Holy Spirit say that as I prayed for the USA that He would open doors for Chris! Just four months later Chris started a new job in Columbus, Ohio!

In April 2005 I visited CIM in Santa Rosa Beach for the Watchman conference and I met Dee at dinner one evening. As we chatted, I discovered that she just happened to live in Mount Vernon, the small town in Ohio where Chris's work was, almost 1,000 miles away! This is my God, a God of surprises and when He orders our steps He does an amazing work.

God further encouraged me through another prophetic word at that conference,

"I will make you to be one who will travel for me and I will open the doors for you to go for me and I will send and I will return and I will send and I will return. I have pulled you back like a catapult ready to be thrusted forth."

While at CIM, Santa Rosa Beach I had heard a wonderful song called "Suddenly" which as soon as I arrived home I ordered the CD. When it arrived it was accompanied by a note saying "felt impressed by God to send you this," which was another CD called "GOD CAN". I sensed the Lord reminding me of Acts 2.2,

Suddenly they heard the sound of a violent blast of wind rushing into the house from out of the heavenly realm

Acts 2:2

Then I heard Him say "It's a time for my Presence to break through, to restore, to build, to bless, and to encourage. I am causing you to be surprised by me, to have your eyes opened and your mind enlarged by my ways."

One month later, I was travelling to Mount Vernon, Ohio to join Chris and see where I was to stay for the next month. Because Chris knew that it was not the best of accommodation, he had bought a huge poster to decorate the back of a door which was covered with the names of God. You can imagine my surprise when I walked in and saw the names of God in front of me.

Shepherd, Advocate, Judge, Master, Lord of Lords, Faithful and True, Rock, Door, High Priest, Living water, True Vine, The Beloved, Good Shepherd, Branch, Mediator, Carpenter, Teacher, Rose of Sharon, Bread of Life. Alpha and Omega, Servant, The Almighty, Chief Cornerstone, Immanuel, Redeemer, Anchor, Bright Morning Star, King of Kings, Lion of the Tribe of Judah and that's not the full list...wow!

This was emphasising that He is my provider, and His provision is perfect. He had given me the perfect friend as well! Dee is now with the Lord in heaven but our times together in Mount

Vernon were fun filled days of stirring up our love for Jesus and together we were like iron sharpening iron.

"As iron sharpens iron, so a man sharpens the countenance of his friend"

Proverbs 27:17

Dee was a lady full of childlike joy who believed that all things were possible, and she knew where to buy the best cheesecakes and eventually found us a really lovely place to stay on the right side of the train tracks!

Nancy and Randy were another God connection in Mount Vernon, they were a couple who briefly worked for Chris and thinking we would not see them again, the last thing I did before we left was pray with Nancy that God would bless them and Randy in their family life, providing them with work for their future. Within a year they had Joined Chris as part of his team on a new contract 2,500 miles away in Portland, Oregon.

Chapter 5

Portland and Oregon

I have always sought the company of other God Chasers and Holy Spirit never fails to lead me to them. I was and still am a 'God Chaser.' I catch the scent of God's presence and want to be there. Tommy Tenney writes in his book "The God Chasers."

> **"God chasers have a lot in common. Primarily they are not interested in camping out on some dusty truth known to everyone. They are after the fresh presence of the Almighty. Sometimes their pursuit raises the eyebrows of the existing church, but usually they lead the church from a place of dryness back into the place of his Presence. If you are a God chaser, you won't be happy to simply follow God's tracks. You will follow them until you apprehend His presence."**

unwittingly embodying that sentiment through and through! Chris had booked my ticket but I did not know that I needed his card to authenticate the booking. The guy on the check in desk would not allow me to travel unless I bought a new ticket! I ran to the ticket counter, bought a new ticket and ran back to the front of the queue to catch my flight, only to be told that I was going to be too late and would not catch that plane.

I **was** getting on that plane!

After much persuasion, of a slightly bemused check in clerk, I suggested that I take my luggage to the departure gate myself. So there I was on a 25 minute sprint across the airport, chasing that flight with no idea about the more God had in store.

Amazingly, I caught the flight and found myself sitting next to the Director of Music from a famous London church. The plane was full of his church members going to a conference in Seattle.

I was so excited to be travelling with a group of hungry Christians who were willing to travel thousands of miles to learn more about Jesus. This magnificent God-incidence had the fingerprint of the Holy Spirit all over it!

During the flight I began to share about a topic of which he previously had little understanding: praying for Israel.

"Pray fervently for the Shalom of Jerusalem! They that love you will have security."

Psalm 122:6 (One New Man Bible.)

It was very exciting to share with him about God's chosen people Israel, that God's covenant is with them forever and that we must pray for the fulfilment of God's plans and purpose for Israel. What was amazing was that it was all new to him! The Apostle Paul says:

"What then? Israel has not obtained what it seeks, but the elect have obtained it, and the rest were blinded; Just as it is written:

God has given them a spirit of stupor, eyes that they should not see and ears that they should not hear, to this very day. And David says 'let their table become a snare and a trap, and a stumbling block, and recompense to them. Let their eyes be darkened so that they do not see and bow down their back always.' I say then, have they stumbled that they should fall? Certainly not! But through their fall to provoke them to jealousy"

Romans 11:7-11.

My fellow traveller said that he had never had anyone explain why he should pray for the Jewish people in a way that he understood. The inspiration went both ways.

I was so stirred by our conversation that the next day I knew I had to go to that Conference. I was also keenly aware that I had just arrived and was fairly sure my husband might raise an eyebrow or two about me heading off solo to a conference that was a three and a half hour drive away. Splendidly, the Lord went before me and prepared Chris's heart: he agreed and he rented a car for me! I had no idea where I was going but had tremendous peace about it all and drove to Seattle by myself with nowhere to stay. Queue in another miracle; the organisers found me accommodation with a local lady. Praise the Lord!

The prophetic and healing conference in Tacoma, at Seattle Revival Centre was a new outpouring of His Spirit. The scent of God's presence had led me there, surrounded by "God Chasers" with deep hearts to serve. By the perfection of God's weaving hand, I was there.

In those two days, I received prophetic prayer to restore years to me–to restore my "original design"– the way God planned for me in my mother's womb. Affirmed, with a vision for the next phase, I departed from the conference. I had eaten a feast of spiritual food which had set me up for the rest of my time in Portland.

It was an awesome start!

Chapter 6

Grace

Chris had promised me that our home in Portland would be a much better standard than our previous one in Ohio and he did not disappoint and I also knew that God was in this work. our apartment was in a beautiful 1900's building in a fabulous neighbourhood and it was called "The Grace". As I have written earlier the best definition of grace for me is, the empowering presence of God, enabling me to be all that He has created me to be and do all that He has created me to do, this was such a timely reminder and promise.

Each time I entered and left the building it was as if I was walking through a double portion of "Grace" as the name was on each side of the steps! It was to be our USA home for the next 3 years .To live and be in a place with such a name was amazing , how wonderful of my Heavenly father to give us such a prophetic place to live in Portland. It was a place of refuge, a place of favour, a place I met with the Lord, worshipping, praying and just sitting. He is the best provider ever!

I was also very excited to meet up with Stuart and Cynthia who I had met in India. They had previously said to me that should I ever be in Portland, that I should visit them – well I did just that. It was so good to see them and they took me to meet their House church friends, who were an amazing group of Intercessors.

Cynthia now is one of my dearest and trusted friends, even today before writing this I have spent an hour speaking to her.

They opened the connection to " street evangelism" led by Ron and Karen Rohman, who gathered two or three times a week in downtown Portland by the Tram stop on Pioneer Courthouse Square (the main shopping area). I joined them and what fun we had sharing the love of God and praying for healing with the passers-by.

Dee (another Dee!) would often join us. She was a lady who at 53 decided to go with Youth with a Mission to Jamaica to help and run all their ministry catering needs. She taught me that it is never too late, or you are never too old to step out in faith! She had a wonderfully large heart for the people who lived on the streets of Portland.

“The Grace” apartment mentioned earlier was in the trendy NW Alphabet district of Portland, with lots of New Age businesses and people.

Prayer and physical cleaning of the streets was needed, each time I have visited the streets were cleaned, it was a physical manifestation of what spiritually was taking place as I walked.

I asked the Lord what He wanted me to do while I was there, and I sensed Holy Spirit say “take my presence everywhere you go, be aware that you carry me into places where I might not be welcomed”, it was simple and I didn't even need to speak but the atmosphere was being changed because God's light always overcomes darkness and he is living in me.

“And the light shines in the darkness and the darkness did not comprehend it. There was a man sent from God whose name was John .... He was not that light; but was sent to bear witness of that light. That was the true Light which gives light to every man coming into the world. “

John 1:5-9

It is often the simplest things that make the most difference; it was simply to be a light shining in the darkness that pointed to THE Light!

I love what Bill Johnson (Senior Leader of Bethel Redding, California) says,

“Our assignment has never been about what we can do for God but what He can do through us “

All I have to do was to be aware that everywhere I went I was a carrier of the Presence of the Lord! And I just needed to be ready for who I might meet and what might happen.

Before leaving the UK on my second visit at the end of 2006, I had booked a Conference at Albany Vineyard church about 80 miles south of Portland and all I had to do was catch a train or so I thought but, trains don't operate there like in the UK. How was I going to get there? I was reminded that Nancy had said “anything I can do to help please ask”. I woke up that morning and heard the Holy Spirit say ask Nancy if you can borrow her car! I asked her and she said yes! I still do not know whether I was insured for driving in the USA. But Holy Spirit made a way for me to hear Chuck Pierce, Apostolic Leader of Glory of Zion, Texas. And Dutch Sheets for the first time.

As I queued to get into the Conference, I started to talk to those around me and met a fabulous couple, Mark and Cathy. One of the brilliant things about travelling and especially to the USA is that the people love the British accent and before we had even got to registration I was urged to go to Bethel Church in Redding California to hear Bill Johnson, then Mark and Cathy went and bought me Bill's book “When Heaven Invades Earth“, a practical guide to a life of miracles. How amazing was that? My heart response was I want to lead a life full of miracles, to see the miracle of salvation as we share the gospel, to see people set free from everything that limits them.

I still have the book and cherish their message to me written on the first page,

"The Spirit of the Lord is upon me, because the Lord has anointed me to ....therefore in their land they will possess the double portion: everlasting JOY shall be for them blessings in the Name of Jesus, Mark and Cathy."

Isaiah 61:1-7,

The Passion translation says,

"The mighty Spirit of Lord Yahweh is wrapped around me because Yahweh has anointed me, as a messenger"

These were such encouraging words for me as I was embarking on this new season in my life. God was saying to me I've wrapped myself around you. I am anointing you, covering and filling you with joyful praise and I am sending you out to preach, heal, bring freedom, bring comfort, console, strengthen, restore, rebuild and repair!!

I could have accepted that morning that I had not planned well enough for this trip, I could have talked my way out of it, and just accepted that I had made a mistake but Holy Spirit was waiting to turn my idea into a tremendous blessing.

Another connection that Holy Spirit connection brought me into was with Vicki who ran Portland Healing Rooms, she and I became great friends and I soon was involved twice a week whenever I was there praying as part of a team for healing and deliverance. We had some wonderful testimonies from folk who turned up for their healing appointments and who left restored, delivered and healed. We were continually amazed at how Holy Spirit led us as we prayed and prophetically guided us. People were hungry for more of the Lord and we were willing channels to be used by Him.

The Lord was showing me that He was and is my provider, " Jehovah Jireh" in every area of my life.

He provided me with friends, who welcomed me to help them in their ministries: friends who were Kingdom connections, friends who sharpened me and opened my eyes to the more of God and friends who were on the same page.

The first mention of God as provider in the Bible,

"Then Abraham lifted up his eyes, and looked and there behind him was a ram caught in a thicket by its horns. So Abraham went and took the ram and offered it up for a burnt offering instead of his son and Abraham called the name of that place, The- Lord-

Will-Provide as it is said to this day, 'In the Mount of the Lord it shall be provided.'"

Genesis 22:13-14.

"Provide" in Hebrew is also "see to it "which is similar to the name Hagar calls the Lord in Genesis 16:13. "The God who sees:" to perceive and experience. The Lord misses nothing, He knows what we need and when we ask He will provide! He knew that I would need friends in Portland and He provided the best!

Vicki was as excited as me when I asked if she would like to go to Bethel Church.

On my next visit to Portland we flew down to Redding and to Bethel Church a group who definitely believe in the supernatural healing power and signs and wonders for today. They train and equip all ages through their Bethel School of Supernatural Ministry. This was another place filled with Joy, where the Kingdom of God was being manifested. Holy Spirit was opening my eyes to an exciting church world where faith to see and a belief for healing and miracles was manifest.

It was here that I saw and heard the amazing Prophets such as Bob Jones, John Paul Jackson, Larry Randolph, Kris Vallotton, Leif Hetland and Lance Wallnau.

I can now see that God was connecting me to Kingdom people, it was so easy to pray there, it was so easy to connect; it was so easy because Holy Spirit was directing my steps.

My visits to Portland became more frequent as my excitement grew for the adventures I was having. Even as I write this I am rereading old journals and can feel the excitement of my time there, such an amazing time of faith building and Holy Spirit leading.

I was made for this!

My prayer at the time was for a cheaper return airline ticket so that I could visit Portland again and the Lord provided! My entry says "I asked the Lord for **favour** for my airline ticket and when I checked it was less than my last trip".

Prophet Sharon Stone had given me a prophecy at my home church in 2005 which was being fulfilled each time I came to Portland.

The Lord says,

"Daughter I am doing some things for you in the area of access. You are a woman who I have given access and liberty, you are going to be able to walk into and out of an environment, not always to stay and build in one place but you will build in other places too. There is an anointing on you to come and go and still build."

I started to realise that it was easy to move between England and the USA and each place and church provided a perfect fit. It always amazed me that when I flew home that it was as if I had missed nothing, spiritually we were all on the same page.

There was such grace on my travels and I was building really deep relationships. At the church that I attended in Portland I met, two amazing ladies, Leslie and Bertie who led a ministry called “Precious daughters.”

They were mother and daughter, and had gone with other ladies to Toronto in the early days of the Toronto outpouring (this was a season when God’s manifest Presence was experienced by thousands of believers who visited the Toronto Airport Church in Canada. It was such a phenomena and it became known as the Toronto Blessing, as much of what was experienced was the Father heart-blessing- of God. Many documented healings and miracles took place at that time and in that place) and each time they were prayed for they were called precious daughters! So the ladies had a new group name of Precious Daughters.

As part of their ministry, they had owned and operated a food van called The Messenger, which they took out each Saturday with a team of helpers to feed the homeless and whenever I was there I jumped at the chance to help them. What a joy to meet these homeless folk, often with such tragic stories but such a privilege to pray, encourage and feed them.

Their ministry was all undergirded by prayer and they met regularly for Holy Spirit encounter nights of worship and prayer, which I had the pleasure of joining. They were all dynamic, lovers of God, full of love and compassion and longed to see God's Kingdom come and His will be done in Portland. Bertie, who is now with the Lord, had known John G Lake (the great healing evangelist) during his ministry in Portland and had seen the signs, wonders, healing and miracles that accompanied his preaching of the gospel. Her faith to see this happen again was infectious!

One of the joys that Chris and I shared was to have Leslie and Bertie join us for Sunday brunch after the church service. We went to our favourite eating place, with its blue and white gingham tablecloths in downtown Portland, where we tucked into blueberry pancakes, cream, syrup and heard more stories from them of their amazing lives.

Chapter 7

Pearl of Great Price

The frantic search for a misplaced pearl is very familiar to me. I have always loved pearls and my engagement ring has two pearls in it, both of which have unfortunately been lost and found a few times.

One time this happened, I was driving Chris to Heathrow Airport. He was flying out to Portland and I noticed that one of the pearls had gone but had no idea where or when I had lost it. I was quite sure that I would find it and enlisted the help of Holy Spirit in that famous four lettered prayer word “HELP”. We searched the car but it was not there. When I returned home a day later, I searched our house, and my clothing, but had to accept that I probably would not find it and we would need to replace the pearl with another. Chris knew how upset I was! All I could think was "Oh Lord, where is it?"

Two days later a very excited Chris called me from Portland to tell me that he had found my pearl! He had opened his computer bag, taken out his computer and heard something drop onto the floor and roll away, it was my pearl! How did it get in there? What were the odds of pulling out his computer in a place where he would hear the pearl drop?

Pearls take many years to be formed and only one in every ten thousand oysters has a pearl in it. They are pieces of hidden treasure waiting to be revealed. Thankfully, Holy Spirit sees the treasure in each one of us and in partnering with Him we get the opportunity to reveal it! Each time a pearl was lost, I prayed and they were found! As precious as those pearls were to me, we are more of a treasure to God than we can ever imagine.

The next time I lost a pearl was in Los Angeles (the city of angels). I was there with Chris, who had gone to a business dinner and left me shopping for the evening. I was wearing my very favourite clip on pearl earrings and I was suddenly aware that one was missing. I was on the pavement outside a shop where I had been trying on a super "poncho" style top and had decided to bring Chris back the following day to see it before I bought it. I frantically searched the pavement, obviously very upset, but no earring. I went back inside and the assistants and I searched everywhere. I had no choice but to abandon my trip and go back to the hotel because I was so upset, but I was reminded of the story of the pearl of great price.

"Heaven's Kingdom realm is also like a jewel merchant in search of rare pearls. When he discovered one very precious and exquisite pearl, he immediately gave up all he had in exchange for it."

Matthew 13:45-46. TPT.

The Passion translation gives the following note on this passage; the Aramaic for precious is "unique". Jesus is the merchant; we, you and I are the exquisite and unique pearl. Jesus discovers where we are hidden, touches us with his love and reveals us as his treasure to a world that needs to find Jesus.

John Wimber, the Leader of the Vineyard movement, gave his life to Jesus when he heard this Scripture being read and said,

"Are you saying that to become a Christian somebody might have to give up everything he has?"

He continued,

"Okay Lord, you can have my career, and it was as though two giant hands came out of heaven and opened my fingers and a voice said 'thank you'."

My story ends with a return to the store on the following morning to look at the poncho and to our amazement as I lifted the first hanger and checked the tag there was my pearl earring hanging from it!

I was so excited that every person in that store heard about the God who loved me so much and so attentively: he had protected my pearl earring. Of course I had to buy the poncho, and every time I wear it, I give thanks to Holy Spirit for the amazing outcome.

Holy Spirit has reminded me of that miracle many times and I have shared that story as I have travelled especially with shop assistants! It has always enabled me to pray with each person, for them to experience the love of God and to know His peace and His Presence. Partnering with Holy Spirit is always fun and full of surprises; it brings the opportunity for God to come into situations where He would not normally be invited.

Chapter 8

Girls Together

An entry in my journal from 2006,

> **"Thank you, Lord, for all my girlfriends in England and the USA. Lord You are so good; You have given me such good friends to stand with me and to encourage me. Each plays such a vital part and together we make up such a force of power, strength and beauty to accomplish much."**

Fran was one of those ladies mentioned. I met Fran at the Watchman Conference in 2002 on my first visit to CIM in Santa Rosa Beach. She was visiting with her friend from Texas, and we were soon chatting and swapping Holy Spirit stories. During one of the breaks, she went off to buy all five Conference books signed by Jane Hamon and Chuck Pierce; all were inscribed to her, but she returned and gave them all to me. I have Jane's book "The Cyrus Decree" in front of me now bearing the inscription to Fran! What a great memory of another God Chaser!

Another great connection was Bonnie. She arrived in Burton in 2008 to help in the church ministry. She joined our team of intercessors and while she was based in town here, she visited my home many times and whilst visiting, she would often play our piano. One particular memorable evening in May 2008, we had returned from a walk in the fields around my village and Bonnie sat down to play. The tune notes of her Holy Spirit led worship consumed me; it filled me, and it ministered to me in a very deep and extraordinary way. It felt as if she had played the story of my life. In October 2023 I heard a teaching from Job,

*"Now yield and submit yourself to Him (**agree** with God and be conformed to His will) and be at peace; in this way (you will prosper and great) good will come to you".*

Job 22:21 (Amplified Bible)

The Greek word for "**agree**" is "*symphoneo*", #4856 in Strong's Concordance. It means to sound together, to be in unison, to be in accord. When we come into harmony with Jesus, releasing His divine Presence, our internal world becomes soothed! When I heard this, I knew in my spirit that Bonnie's Holy Spirit led piano playing had done this. Spirit to spirit she had found the place of agreement with Jesus's story in my life. As I have read and reread my journals spanning 20 years, I am gaining amazing insight into my Holy Spirit adventures.

Someone who encouraged me so much in prayer was Ginny Marks. She was an intercessor who travelled on international prayer assignments with Chuck Pierce as part of the Eagles of God prayer team. I had the joy of prayer supporting her many times as she travelled. I remember her and give thanks for her every time I see the words "mind the gap" on the London underground. Ginny had written a pamphlet titled "Mind the Gap" on intercession based on the scripture,

"So I sought for a man among them who would make a wall, and stand in the gap before Me on behalf of the land, that I should not destroy it; but I found no one."

Ezekiel 22:30

Many years before on one of our KAN Prayer journeys to Rome a dear friend, Anji, had given all the team a bookmark she had made with a single rose on the top and the words,

"Listen, daughter, and pay careful attention...Let the king be enthralled by your beauty; honour him, for he is your Lord."

Psalm 45:10, 11 (NIV)

She had led us in a devotional one morning using it and I had treasured this and decided to get some printed and give them away to any young women I met. It started the creation of more bookmarks to give away and soon another followed,

"You're beautiful from head to toe, my dear love, beautiful beyond compare, absolutely flawless."

Song of Songs 4:7 (the Message Bible)

My heart was moved by the many heavily tattooed and homeless young women that I met, who had no idea of how beautiful they were and who were struggling with their identity. I was drawn to them. I wanted to give them something personal to take away. Jesus had revealed to me how much He loved me all those years ago and I wanted to do the same for these young women who did not know that they were loved by Him! Stasi Eldredge in her book "Captivating" writes,

"Just as Cinderella was invited to the ball, God is inviting you to a great romance with Him. The eyes of His heart are ever upon you, the King is captivated by your beauty."

When we give our testimony of what God has done for us, we are being authentic. It's not just theory or something we have read; it is real. I just loved to stop, talk, listen and sit with these ladies who lived on the streets and leave them with a bookmark that reminded them that they were loved. As I write this, I am so aware that the cry of all of our hearts is to be loved.

My darling speaks; He is saying to me,
"Get up my love! My beauty! Come away!"
Song of Songs 2:10 (CJB)

A friend who I shared many adventures with was Sue. Sue and I had met in our local village store in 1983, shortly after Chris and I had moved into our house. It was a God moment but at that time neither of us were born again believers, but He had started the journey for us both of discovering Jesus and His plan for our lives.

Sue's ministry is focused and mostly centred on reaching and ministering to women and she suggested that we attend the annual "Colour" conference hosted by Hillsong UK at Wembley, London in November 2004.

I believe that God's timing is perfect and one of the memorable talks that are noted in my journal was titled "She is no ordinary girl".

I wrote,

- **God was emphasising that there was a call on my life; I was not to be seduced by the ordinary.**

· God wanted to strengthen in me the qualities of the extraordinary.

· I was created as a helper; one who comes alongside; who stands in the gap, then moves on.

· With an unyielding pioneering spirit, I was going into uncharted territory to make a way for others, with 100% commitment to complete what God has entrusted me with.

· I am a woman who pushes through my personal boundaries.

· I am marked for the Father's business, to see things as He sees them, to see His master plan. That my eyes would view life differently, looking beyond the natural.

God's promise for us all is that we are emerging as ones perfected in identity, authority and dignity. The Proverbs 31 Woman! A Warrior; A princess; A daughter.

We came home with the most amazing t-shirts with this inscribed on them,

"Warrior Princess Daughter
"She smiles at the future,
Lives life magnificently,
Executes justice on the earth,
And places value on humanity."

Sue flew out to visit me many times whilst I was in the USA, and together with Holy Spirit, we went wherever He led us. It was so much fun and so easy to pray with people whether we were shopping, eating, walking, or sightseeing: we were wide eyed with excitement every time Holy Spirit touched people's lives through us.

One of my favourite memories with Sue was at a *Christian International* Conference in 2005. We had rented a small apartment near the beach. It wasn't the nicest of places, but it was a place to rest our heads. In my journal entry I write that we had had the most amazing early morning prayer and encounter times in this small apartment.

Dee was at the same Conference and when she heard about our bijoux apartment, she insisted we move in with her as she had a beautiful house with lots of space and she wanted to bless us, and she did.

Meeting Nancy Veldman was another great blessing to us. She owned a beautiful lifestyle store just down the road and the centrepiece of the store was a grand piano. The music she played came straight from heaven and had such a healing anointing on it! Her gift of playing was totally reliant on Holy Spirit, as she had started to play after her father died and had experienced her own healing through it.

Sue also joined me in Portland in 2009 to visit Bethel Church in Redding, and we decided to embark on an 8-hour drive to get there! We planned a coffee stop, trusting Holy Spirit to lead us to a good one and we found it! It was a donut trucker cafe in a small community where each person and regular trucker had their own mug hanging from the wall.

We ended up meeting everyone, hearing their stories and praying for this dear elderly couple who asked if we could call on our return journey to see them. Five days later we stopped, and we were there waiting for them. This is the God I love, who loves people so much that He plans divine appointments for them to be touched by His love, and He used us as willing vessels to do it! Of course, we prayed for them to know that love in that cafe. Once again two ordinary ladies were used by an extraordinary God to reveal His love.

I love sharing my experiences with others, which is why I am writing this book. So, in the spring of 2010 Sue and I decided to go back to Bethel, Redding for a conference; this time taking others with us who had never done anything like this before! Suzanne, another Sue and my sister-in-law Irene, joined us. We called it the Awesome Women's Tour. We flew into San Francisco and hired a car to drive to Redding with of course a short detour to shop!

As we registered for the Conference there was excitement as they realised that Irene's home was in Wales, but she was also living and working with her husband in Gibraltar. They had never had visitors from Gibraltar before, especially with a Welsh connection. (The Welsh Revival of 1904 affected the world when the Spirit of God descended on a young peoples' prayer meeting setting their hearts on fire for more of Jesus and they then went around the local churches to share the blessing resulting in 130,000 people being saved). As a result, we had seats saved for us each day. We experienced an amazing honour as international visitors, and favour followed us wherever we went.

My journal entry from the 17th of July 2011 reminded me that Suzanne and I were together in Jerusalem. We had been to Israel sightseeing with KAN the previous year (and, many years since introducing new people to the Land) and both wanted to return to spend more time praying but we also wanted to walk the walls of Jerusalem, which we had started but not finished.

We took the shuttle bus from Tel Aviv airport to Jerusalem and met a young woman on the journey who was returning to *Succat Hallel*, one of the Houses of Prayer in Jerusalem, after renewing her visa. What was remarkable and an amazing Holy Spirit connection was that she had been staying with Anji (the friend who had given me the bookmark) and it was one of the Houses of Prayer that we were planning to visit on that very trip. The next morning, we were at *Succat Hallel* at the 10-12pm prayer time led by the leader Rick Ridings. We were praying for the Mediterranean Sea and all the countries around it. Suddenly someone began to pray about the UK presence in the Mediterranean through Gibraltar. My journal reads,

"I was stunned as my brother Peter was Captain of the Port and his job was running and watching over the comings and goings of this very important strategic port and I had been praying all week for them to walk in their destiny in that place where the Spirit of Islam has many times tried to break through. Suzanne and I had even been praying for them and had telephone them with a prophetic word from Suzanne for Irene at the airport before we flew out!"

Interestingly the name Gibraltar comes from an Arabic name meaning conqueror. As we had experienced in Bethel with Irene, Gibraltar was on God's heart, and He was calling us to pray.

The next morning, we were back again at *Succat Hallel* as they were praying for the UK! Holy Spirit was leading us step by step to be where we needed to be at the right time.

We walked the walls on the following day and as we went through the Old City, we stopped to look at pashmina shawls and entered into conversation with the Armenian seller about Jesus. After several visits to him that week, we led him to the Lord, and he gave us each a pashmina!

In 2019 on the last business trip for Chris and I to Vancouver Island, Canada, I met Karen Scott and Cathy Coulson who together with a small team lead a House of Prayer in Gibsons west of Vancouver. They were another key connection!

Back home at KAN we had connected with some prayer leaders in Australia: Peter and Kathryn Yaxley who were going to Canada in September 2018 and wanted to visit KAN enroute and stay with me. I was intrigued by their prayer assignment as it was going through the very town where Chris was working in Vancouver Island, so I asked if I could support them in prayer. Once again, Holy Spirit had made an amazing connection for me. It was fun to be part of their team, even at a distance, because Holy Spirit is the best team builder.

When I did meet Karen and Cathy, it just happened to be for the Feast of Tabernacles, which we celebrated together with their team, and I was the honoured guest! In the first few moments of meeting them I knew this was a very special God connection because we started to talk about the Bride of Christ, and I burst into tears. A longing for more of Jesus had been growing in me since I had been part of the House of Prayer at Catch the Fire, CTF (formerly Toronto Airport Church) and my visit to IHOPKC in Kansas City. Karen and Cathy's language tied spiritual warfare to intimacy and the celebration of the Hebraic feast. We had the most amazing three days together:

worshipping, praying, feasting and laughing. Holy Spirit had led me to more of my tribe.

I joined them in a 180-day Bible reading plan in April the following year which they called Relentless: 180 Degrees.

"What is 180 Degrees? It is a 180-day pilgrimage that sends you out to abide in and respond to the reality of God's love and holy presence. The path is holy and walked out in true worship in spirit and in truth. It begins with your expressed love and desire for the Lord and His Presence, but only true humility and courage will take you down the path to where your heart burns with holy fear to become a resting place for the Lord. This time is a relentless pursuit of the Lord Jesus, liken it to a betrothal. Keep in mind, as you draw near Him you will be transformed."

This is what I have been trying to do over the last three years, intentionally responding to the Lord's love and His greatest desires for me, willingly turning away from anything that would try to separate me from Jesus, the lover of my soul.

As I write this in January 2024 and I look back at my journey since then, I am reminded that Chuck Pierce talked about us entering a War Season from September 2019 that would take us through the next decade.

Chuck says, "this is the ERA to come face to face with the enemy and also with God!" The above does not look like war, but I believe Holy Spirit was establishing an abiding, resting place in me for Him to fully dwell, where I would meet with God and where I would war from!

The word of God when it opens up is alive and is filled with light. It is vital as times become darker that we feed on the word of God.

"Arise; shine; for your light has come! And the glory of the Lord is risen upon you. For behold the darkness shall cover the earth. And deep darkness the people; But the Lord will arise over you and His glory will appear upon you."

Isaiah 60:1-2

Chapter 9

The God My Healer

Praying for the sick to be healed should be part of our normal everyday life as Christians and that includes praying for ourselves. John G. Lake, the great healing evangelist who had been sent by God to Africa in 1908, believed that Spirit filled Christians should enjoy the same type of ministry Jesus did while living on earth and that this reality could only be accomplished by seeing themselves as God sees them. In 2007, I had to believe for my own healing.

Towards the end of 2007, I visited my doctor who flagged up a potential problem with my heart; its rhythm was erratic, and she referred me to a cardiologist. My mother had a heart problem and it had been suggested that this could be an inherited family disease. It was time to pray and remind myself of who I was and whose I was: a daughter of my heavenly Father with His DNA. I was not accepting that diagnosis.

Since the day I accepted God as my Father and was born again, all my past was renewed, and every inherited disease was no longer mine! The Kingdom of heaven does not have sickness, therefore as a part of that Kingdom, I decided I was going to trust in the Lord to heal my heart.

Jesus did everything out of a relationship with His heavenly Father and He says to us that we will do greater things.

"Most assuredly I say to you, he who believes in me, the works that I do, he will do also; and greater works than these he will do, because I go to My Father."

John 14:12

Jesus chose to live as a man on earth to show us how it is possible for us to live in His supernatural power! We have a long way to go to ever live like Jesus did, but that must be our benchmark.

The day to visit the cardiologist arrived and his first words to me as I walked into his room were, "I do not know why you have come, as there is nothing wrong with you" and then he said, "Whatever affected your family, you have escaped the genetics of the past"! He then examined me and suggested, just to make sure, that I had an echocardiogram, an ultrasound of the heart.

As I waited for it at the hospital, I started to read Acts 3 and was reading the story of the beggar at the Gate Beautiful, who was healed! It was verse 16 that Holy Spirit highlighted,

*"And on the basis of faith in His name, it is the name of Jesus that has strengthened this man whom you see and know and the faith which comes through him has given him this **perfect health** in the presence of you all."*

(NAS Bible)

The lady carrying out the ultrasound examination had a student with her and she talked and explained to the student as she looked at the whole of my heart and she ended by saying I had a "perfect heart".

Wow, what a God! He amazes me: I know that my God and Father healed me that day!

John Wimber, leader of Vineyard Church, had influenced me greatly when he testified about praying for healing in his church every week for two years before seeing healing take place and then he saw healings every week!

"If you will diligently heed the voice of the Lord your God, and will do what is right in His sight, give ear to His commandments, and keep all His statutes, I will put none of the diseases on you, which I have brought on the Egyptians: for I AM the Lord that heals you."

Exodus 15:26,

In the New Testament,

"Men of Israel hear these words: Jesus of Nazareth, a Man attested by God to you by miracles, wonders, and signs which God did through Him in your midst..."

Acts 2:22,

Jesus only did what He saw His father doing,

"Most assuredly I say to you, the son can do nothing of Himself, but what He sees the Father do; for whatever He does, the son also does in like manner".

John 5:19

Like Jesus, out of our relationship with the Father, we can do what He did and greater things. Whenever I visited Portland, I was able to be part of the team at the Healing Rooms, started by John G. Lake. Upon his return to the USA from his powerful missionary movement in Africa, he established Healing Rooms, in Spokane and in Portland, where hundreds and hundreds of people were healed by the power of God. Now **Healing Room Ministries** are all over the world. He was a man of tremendous faith whose story inspired me to believe for more and it was a joy to pray for people to be healed. I did and still love praying for people: I love seeing their surprised faces; I love their response when they feel His Presence. I love seeing the same God who healed my heart, touching others' lives and healing today.

Chapter 10

Going to the Nations

In April 2009 I arrived in Kampala, Uganda with KAN leaders Dit and Howard McCallum, along with some very excited young people from our church. What was Holy Spirit leading us into?

Passion for Jesus Ministries (PFJ) led by the amazing Mark Curtis, had inspired us to make the journey and introduced us to some of his contacts there, but of course the Lord also made some new connections for us too.

This was to be a visit marked by prayer on the mountain tops!

We had travelled in a very old bus with diesel fumes coming through the window next to me, so when we arrived our faces were covered in sooty black diesel deposits. Pastors Mary and Duncan Kibaya, our fabulous, joy filled hosts in Masaka at **River**

of Life Church, whisked us off to clean us up and just love on us before taking us up to their Prayer Mountain. This was land that was in Duncan's family and set aside for prayer.

"For the land which you go to possess is not like the land of Egypt from which you have come, where you sowed your seed and watered it by foot, as a vegetable garden, but the land which you cross over to possess is a land of hills and valleys, which drinks water from the rain of heaven, a land for which the Lord your God cares; the eyes of the Lord your God are always on it, from the beginning of the year to the very end of the year."

Deuteronomy 11:10-12

I had taken some thyme from my garden and as a prophetic act we scattered it on the land and declared,

"It is God's time: time for blessings to flow, time for healings, time for deliverance, and time for the wells to be re-dug. It's time for the earth to release its harvest."

We were aware that we were strategically positioned on the Equator and as we looked North, South, East and West we were reminded of God's Word to Joshua,

"Every place that the sole of your foot will tread upon, I have given you."

Joshua 1:3

It was such a privilege to stand alongside the local people and pray for more of God's Kingdom to be released in their nation, to encourage them, to know that wherever we go, God takes our offering of "loaves and fishes" and works His miracle. I am so overwhelmed by the great God we serve who plans every footstep and every word we speak when we give Him our lives!

We left Masaka to meet with Pastor Michael Kimuli in Kampala at **Christian Discipleship Ministries**. We met in his office on Good Friday where he was so overwhelmed that a group of young people had travelled to pray for Uganda and the Nations.

We had an amazing time of prayer with Pastor Michael; we prayed for the release of the Prophetic in the nation and nations. We prayed for dry bones to come to life and a water bottle fell onto my feet! My journal says,

"I cannot describe the power we felt in that room, but if we have come to Uganda for just this, it has been worth it, wow! I know we must release the prophetic word wherever we go, over the land; over the people."

We saw in the spirit a mountain erupting like a volcano and interpreted it as a sign that God is pouring forth His presence in power on the nation, and we called forth the Ugandan church to catch the fire again!

We knew that we had all come from a church of fire starters, so we were carrying a flame to rekindle fires, calling on the church to not give up when they and we were so close to breakthrough. Pastor Michael was working with Pastor John Mulinde, from **World Trumpet Mission** who had set up **Nations Prayer Mountain**, just outside Kampala, after a time of Christian persecution during the reign of President Idi Amin. Their website says,

> **"After the freedom to pray was regained, we built the Nations Prayer Mountain as a 24 hour Altar, interceding for all the Nations of the world as a way to express our thankfulness to the people that stood in prayer with Uganda."**

Michael's book "Effective Fervent Prayer" says,

> **'The Lord gave John a strategy for preparing the Nation for revival. It was from Genesis 12-13, where Abraham used altars to take Canaan, the promise to him and his descendants. The Lord told John to use the same strategy, to "build me a net of prayer so that I can fish the nation out of troubled waters"'.**

This was another amazing place to pray: one of those thin places where we released prophetic words, worshipped together in an open sided church, where people from all over the world come for up to a month to camp and pray.

Our young people led the service that night, speaking on the power of the Holy Spirit and leading many to speak in tongues for the first time. One of our girls Sarah had been prayed for by Pastor Michael earlier that day for a gift of healing to be released. She led the prayer for healing that night and amazingly is now a qualified doctor!

We prayed for many people in Uganda. One was Netti, a young completely deaf girl who was healed in her right ear. We had prayed twice to get complete healing: she started crying as we pressed in for healing in her left ear because she could hear. She gave her life to the Lord as we all cried and gave thanks to our amazing God.

One of the communities we visited was in Mbale, which took six to seven hours to drive to. Fourteen of us and our luggage were packed into a very small bus and then with two hours still to go, in true African style, we picked up two more people. If we felt cramped before we certainly did now.

At the time of our visit, many villages had no running water and no electricity, yet it was beautiful: the hillsides were very well cultivated, the pace of life was very slow yet there was much to do. Water took hours to collect, and clothes were washed in rainwater collected in a muddy hole. We stayed in Buwesunguyi, where money given by our church had enabled the village to have a health centre. Our greeting upon arrival was amazing: the school children sang, and the mothers had cooked a feast of omelettes, meat and rice followed by fresh pineapples and bananas, which tasted wonderfully sweet and a million miles away from what we get in the UK! We were blessed by these beautiful people who had to carry every inch of water up the hill just to look after us!

It makes no sense to me that the people were so poor, yet the land was so fertile, and the weather was good. Life was hard yet it was so simple and beautiful. Everything was cooked for us over an open fire in a room with no ventilation, yet these people were full of such love: they served us with open hearts and hands. The Bishop had moved out of his house to give us rooms and beds to sleep in and we found him sleeping on the floor with his wife, children and two servants! What a humbling and blessed experience. Despite having so little, they gave and gave and gave. We left knowing that we had been truly blessed.

Chapter 11

Canada

In October 2010, Chris was contacted by a Canadian company who needed his expertise for two years in Barrie, Ontario, a Town 75 miles north of Toronto and he agreed. We were to leave for Canada at the end of August 2011 to begin the work.

The timing of leaving was also in the Biblical month of Elul, when traditionally the King came out of His palace and met His people in the field. Elul is a special month and time to draw near to God with the revelation of His nearness to us. In the Bible, King Jehoshaphat went "into the field" and this proximity allowed him to effectively restore peoples' hearts back to God.

"So Jehoshaphat dwelt at Jerusalem: and he went out again among the people from Beer-sheba to the mountains of Ephraim, and brought them back unto the Lord God of their fathers"

2 Chronicles 19:4

Just before I left I had written in my journal, "I ask you Lord, is there any part of my life that I have not put in your hands? I will approach you; I will meet with you in your tent this month to receive your strength to proceed in the month ahead."

I wanted to be in Gods timing for the next season of my life.

As we flew out I pondered on the work of Holy Spirit in preparing for this day, I was taken back to February 2010 at Bethel Church, Redding when John Arnott, the leader of **Catch the Fire** (CTF) Toronto was speaking. I heard Holy Spirit say "do you want to go to that man's church?" My heart leapt and said YES! God had answered my heart cry.

It did not take long for me to start to drive to CTF on a regular basis as I sensed that I was to be part of the church family there and I realised why I prayed that prayer before I came.

I soon learnt to drive on a six lane highway, read foreign road signs at speed, drive on the wrong side of the road, use cruise control, drive lots of different cars and enjoy the journey of a round trip of 150 miles each time and well worth the drive. The month of Elul is also a time of harvest and I was reaping the fruit of answered prayer. Eighteen months after I said **YES** to Holy Spirit asking me if I wanted to go to **Catch the Fire**, I was given a fantastic welcome and invited to join their Intercessors!

A month later at a CTF conference called "Convergence" that I found myself ministering to a lady as she lay resting with Holy Spirit and she opened her eyes and said, "Have you written a book?" "No!" was my reply. She had no idea why she said it, but later I asked the Lord, "what am I to write about?" He replied "your story of journeys with me!!!" I am shocked as I write this as I did not remember that. I wonder how much we forget about things that fill us with fear. But our wonderful God never forgets and wants us to accomplish our full potential.

One of the characteristics of Catch the Fire was their teaching on the "Father Heart of God "and it was foundational. They knew God as Father and everything that was taught was from that place.

Their mission statement was,

"That we may walk in God's love and then give it away"

Marc Dupont who was on staff at *CTF* during the Toronto Blessing said,

"You have made CTF a resting place for God"

The Lord said that he would release grace to walk in Song of Songs 8:6-7 across the body of Christ worldwide and that Mike was to focus on this theme throughout his ministry. Mike says after initially being intimidated by the language, he began to find much delight and pleasure in studying it as he encountered Jesus the Bridegroom and felt the power of His love.

I was to experience that during my time there.

Knowing that we had rented our home with a cleaner for 3 months and I had no housework to do focused my mind so I planned to study Mike Bickles' (former Leader of International House of Prayer Kansas City) 24 session study of "Song of Songs".

In his introduction to the study Mike shares of hearing the audible voice of God as he was reading Song of Songs 8:6 and began to pray

"Let Jesus seal my heart with the seal of His love"

"Fasten me upon your heart as a seal of fire forever, this living, consuming flame will seal you as a prisoner of love. My passion is stronger than the chains of death and the grave, all consuming as

the very flashes of fire from the burning heart of God. Place this fierce, unrelenting fire over your entire being. Rivers of pain and persecution will never extinguish this flame. Endless floods will be unable to quench this raging fire that burns within you. Everything will be consumed. It will stop at nothing as you yield everything to this furious fire until it won't even seem to you like a sacrifice anymore."

Song of Songs 8:6-7 TPT

I agree when Mike Bickle says Song of Songs reveals Gods pattern in how we grow in passion for Jesus.

For 3 months I was immersed in Jesus' revelation of love for his bride and the Fathers love for us as His children!

Once again the Lord provided me with amazing friends. I was able to join a *CTF* cell group, led by Sharon Coates who lived in Alliston, just down the road from where we lived. Those ladies were a joy to be with, I pinch myself at the goodness of God and the connections He had for me. They were a power house of prayer, a furnace of prayer, where they poured out their hearts on behalf of others. Their prayers and resulting authority in Holy Spirit was blessing the area. They were a torch of love covering the town of Alliston. Not only did we share Jesus, but we shared life together and I learnt so much about their lives and how one does life in Canada. What Canadian homes are like, potluck suppers, visiting cottage country (weekend retreats in the forest) and quilting. I am now the proud owner of an amazing patchwork quilt made by my wonderful cell group friend, Nancy Snook.

CTF had just started a House of Prayer modelled on the 24/7 International House of Prayer in Kansas City, which I had heard about when we lived in Portland. It was led by Patricia Bootsma, who with her husband John was Pastoring *CTF*, involving many of the school of ministry students. I've always loved being with young people whose hearts are on fire for Jesus and it was such a joy to stand alongside them and pray as their worship was passionate, exciting and fresh.

As I read through my journals, I am amazed by so many references to "fear".

Kris Vallotton, one of the Senior Leaders of Bethel church Redding, says,

"Fear is the faith in the wrong God, the only fear we should have as believers is the fear of the Lord.

"The fear of the Lord is the beginning of wisdom"
Proverbs 9:10. KJV

My involvement in The House of Prayer at *CTF* as a prayer leader was another opportunity for fear to try to stop me, it's that voice in our ears that says, what if you dry up, make a mistake, da, da, da..... But as I wrote at the time, when fear is exposed it can be dealt with and I had amazing friends to help me! We were a team, there were singers, musicians, and of course Holy Spirit.

The Lord had promised me His strength.

"My grace is enough; it's all you need. My strength comes into its own in your weakness"

2 Corinthians 12:10 (The Message Bible)

One of the first steps in walking in the Fear of the Lord is learning to trust in Him!

I love praying for the nations and especially when I am in the Nation, so being in Canada and praying for Canada was such a privilege.

"Even them I will bring to My holy mountain and make them joyful in My house of prayer: their burnt offerings and their sacrifices will be accepted upon My altar; For My house shall be called a house of prayer for all nations"

Isaiah 56:7

Chris and I were blessed by our time in Canada; many told me that the Canadian church would become a healing to other nations. The flag of Canada is a maple leaf and scripture states:

"The leaves of the tree were for the healing of the nations
"Revelation 22:2

We were blessed by many people, Lucy and Julia, mother and daughter who owned a lovely restaurant in Barrie called Arabesque, sadly it has closed since, but we enjoyed many evenings of wonderful Lebanese food and their generous hearts drew us to love them.

One of my favourite day time stops was "Simply Tea & Chocolate" run by Susie, who gave me a free lunch and a big hug the day I left!

Crystal Parrott, a great friend I met at *CTF*, introduced us to the world of healthy eating, of "date balls" and "Kale crisps" (made from dehydrated kale!) Her business based on Nutrition and essential oils was a great blessing to us and we shared some amazing prayer, conversations and family times together.

The lady next door said that her headaches had diminished since prayer and hugs! I wrote in my journal, "Lord you have blessed me beyond anything I expected".

I came across a key prophetic word from Glory of Zion in October 2011 that said, "The field that you thought you would go into at the beginning of the year is not the field or the gate that I am opening for you. You have sown seeds of righteousness in the past season that has been held to bring forth in this season"

I had expected to be part of the evangelism teams, because of the outreach we were doing at *KAN* when I went to *CTF* but I spent most of my time supporting Prayer and Intercession.

When I asked the Lord He said, "I needed you to help support and prepare and position my church in CTF for advancing in the Kingdom in the next season".

This was another wonderful season and I began to move almost seamlessly between *CTF* and *KAN*. I never missed out; spiritually I was flowing in the same river!!

CTF was a magnet for some of the "great" preachers that I was privileged to hear, RT Kendall; Jack Taylor; Duncan Smith; Charles Carrin; James Maloney and Heidi Baker, to name just a few.

Duncan Smith, who is now President of *Catch the Fire World*, signed for me his book "Consumed by Love" with the words, **"May your shadow be absolutely saturated with the presence and power of God, just as your body is"**

I believe that we are entering those times written about in the book of Acts 5.15

"When people knew Peter was going to walk by, they carried the sick out to the streets and laid them down on cots and mats, knowing the incredible power emanating from him would overshadow them and heal them"

Jesus was challenging me to do my part, it was as if He was saying, "I won't if you don't, but I will if you will!" It reminds me of praying for someone at lunchtime during one of our prayer days. Actually I was not praying but demonstrating the "Hunter Technique" of praying for unequal length legs! And it turned into a healing. As I demonstrated I mixed up the legs and the wrong leg grew and I shouted "no Lord it's the wrong leg, but it was the right leg! He knew and He showed me that it's not about us! But His grace covers us AND God did a miracle.

I was blessed richly with the friends who visited us from the UK, who I introduced to *CTF*. Sue had joined us in Portland, had visited Bethel with me and came out to Canada.

One of the stories, and there were many! She was with me when we had a car accident in snowy weather on our way to church, no real damage to us but the car needed help. The pickup truck driver who came to collect us, who we quickly got to know, was an Assyrian Christian from Iraq. His wife, Aliza, telephoned him, during the telephone conversation Sue had a prophetic word for her, which she shared with our driver, who handed her the phone to talk to his wife. Aliza cried as Sue shared the Lord's word to her, it was an answer to the conversation she had had with the Lord earlier in the day. He had heard the cry of her heart! And answered in a miraculous way!

Chapter 12

Outreach and Evangelism

One of the things I loved when we were living in Portland was praying with people for healing and talking about Jesus on the streets, so I was very excited to try and do this when I was back in my home church of KAN. Stephen and Jenny, the KAN leaders, encouraged us to get outside of the church walls to share our faith and the young people at KAN were especially willing to pray with people in order to develop their prophetic skills.

We started going into the town sharing to anyone who was open to hear from us, encouraging words from God who was speaking through us: we called them "Whispers from Heaven", Our Pastor, David, a photographer, helped us by taking various photos of scenes, people, and buildings, which we laminated and then pegged onto a mobile line. We then took them with us into our local town of Burton, where we asked passers-by to select an image from the photos, which we used to speak an encouraging word to them from God. As an example a photo of two clasped hands was chosen, we prayed asking Holy Spirit for a relevant and encouraging word such as,

"I hear Holy Spirit say to me now, 'As you put your hand into mine, know precious one that I will not let you go, for I will lead you every step of the way, into a future you could never have imagined.'"

This was often followed by, "How did you know?" We were often astonished at the way Holy Spirit communicated with the people we met.

I had been encouraged to try this at Bethel Church when we heard about "Treasure Hunting", this is simply asking the Lord to show us before heading into town, who we might meet, with visible specifics about them, such as what they were wearing or any disability limitations. Bethel was not just a place to hear but it was a place to do and be activated. In other words, to have a go! Someone once said that the church has become constipated because we have had too much teaching and have stopped going!

Kevin Dedmon led us out onto the streets of Redding to practice. We had so much fun with Holy Spirit that we all returned home with his wonderful book, The Ultimate Treasure Hunt: A Guide to Supernatural Evangelism through Supernatural Encounters.

Bill Johnson says in the Foreword,

"This book brings both Evangelism and the gifts of the Spirit into such a beautiful union... it's a way of life that Holy Spirit makes available to everyone...to be put into the hands of hungry people who would become equipped to make a difference in the world around them."

Kevin's stories encouraged us when I returned home to Burton on Trent to go out on "treasure hunts" to find the hidden treasure: people who the Holy Spirit was leading us to. One of my favourite phrases was (using the analogy of the National Lottery) the giant hand of God is pointing to you today to tell you how much He loves you.

We would often have people come up to us asking, "Please can we be the treasure?" because they wanted to receive an encouraging word.

"But a life lived loving God bears lasting fruit, for the one who is truly wise wins souls"

Proverbs 11:30, TPT

As I am writing this my current reading book is "Prophetic Forecast" by Joshua Giles. The following is a quote from the chapter titled Supernatural Harvest on page 145.

The Spirit told me to focus on the word "win", which in Hebrew is lāqah: to accept and to receive. So, the text is saying he who receives and accepts souls is wise! It is not our job to save people, Jesus does the saving. God said "Don't ask people if they are Christians. Don't ask them if they go to church, just speak my words, and leave them to me." I was brought up in a church environment where we witnessed to people with pamphlets and booklets outlining the Gospel message and had a prearranged set of questions to ask them. That was the old wineskin. The new methodology is Spirit led evangelism. The gifts of the Holy Spirit must be front and centre when ministering to the lost. Many people will not come to God unless He reveals the secrets of their hearts and He wants to talk to people in this way, using me and you to do it.

I am excited as I read Joshua's prophetic book as he finishes that section with the words,

"The next great awakening is coming through prophetic evangelism."

Holy Spirit has been teaching and preparing you and me for this very time in history.

"All authority has been given to Me in heaven and on earth. Go therefore and make disciples of all the nations, baptising them in the name of the Father, and of the Son and of the Holy Spirit, teaching them to observe all things that I have commanded you; and lo I am with you always , even to the end of the age."

Matthew 28:18-20

Chapter 13

IHOP Kansas City

My heart was crying out for "one thing."

"One thing I have desired of the Lord that I will seek; that I may dwell in the house of the Lord all the days of my life, to behold the beauty of the Lord, and to inquire in His temple."

Psalm 27:4

In June 2013, we found ourselves back at home in Staffordshire preparing for our youngest son, Tim's, wedding thinking we would be at home for an English summer when another telephone call changed that, and I was on my way to IHOPKC Chris was needed back in Toronto for at least a month and amazingly we were able to book great value flights via Kansas City for me and direct to Canada for Chris. How many times can

I testify of the Lord going before me and making a way? One of my favourite songs is Way Maker,

"Way maker, miracle worker, promise keeper, light in the darkness, my God that is who You are...Even when I don't see it, You're working, even when I don't feel it, You're working, You never stop, You never stop working"

"God the searcher of the heart knows fully our longings, yet He also understands the desires of the spirit, because the Holy Spirit passionately pleads before God for us, His holy ones, in perfect harmony with God's plan and our destiny. So, we are convinced that every detail of our lives is continually woven together to fit into God's perfect plan of bringing good into our lives, for we are His lovers who have been called to fulfil his designed purpose"

Romans 8:27-28 (TPT)

We were able to rent the perfect apartment in the perfect location and it was perfect timing for me to attend a 10-day "Immerse" course at IHOPKC Fortunately, there was space on the course for me! My accommodation was sorted as well because one of the leaders at Catch the Fire, Toronto, Canada had a house there and they had a spare room to rent! Not only that but when I arrived at the airport, I had been given an upgrade and was travelling business class!

About "Immerse", the IHOPKC website says,

"Come and experience five days of inspiring teaching, ministry times, fasting and, most of all, the presence of God in our global prayer room in which prayer with worship has been going nonstop since 1999."

Each monthly "Immerse" had a different emphasis and July's was led by Corey Stark and was called "Restoring the Family". It could not have been a more perfect subject for me. My heart has always been to see my whole family knowing Jesus one day, and to see broken families restored.

"Your people will rebuild long deserted ruins, building anew on foundations laid long before you. You will be known as repairers of the cities and restorers of communities (or restorers of paths that lead you home)"

Isaiah 58:12 (TPT)

Corey always led but it was to be the first time on the course that he shared how God had restored his marriage. It was an amazing testimony and his wife joined him to share her version of the miracle. I had no idea, but this amazing testimony was to build faith in me for the future, for me to believe that a family marriage could be restored ... and it was.

We were immersed for five days in the life of IHOPKC: each of us was given daily two-hour prayer times in the Global Prayer Room as well as our teaching and gathering times. Worship at IHOPKC is foundational. There has been 24/7 prayer taking place for 24 years, with constant worship in two-hour sessions. It is unique; it was such a privilege to be part of such an anointed community of all ages.

As part of the emphasis on restoration, my group went to visit a restoration project run by IHOPKC called Hope City, which was a House of Prayer and community centre working in the inner city of Kansas City. They were seeing lives rebuilt and restored out of addiction and people set free, a place full of possibilities and hope. Our bus driver just happened to be called Chris Smith! It was so encouraging especially when someone prophesied to me, "You are being driven in your ministry by Chris to a place of hope in the midst of darkness. Chris is leading the way"

The amazing thing is that I know that! So much that I have experienced is because my wonderful husband has enabled me to do it.

My last morning at IHOPKC started early with a session in the prayer room. A coffee outside led me to chat with Debbie, a lady with an awesome testimony. We prayed, we loved, and we laughed together. She shared with me stories of manna falling from heaven onto her kitchen floor; her dancing in the Spirit with a rag, flinging it against the wall and seeing that a picture had been painted of an oil lamp lit with a flame. She had an encounter with joy! It was such a delight to meet another of my Heavenly Father's children! This was another divine experience of being in the right place at the right time. I know that Holy Spirit brought us together; we left encouraged, excited and uplifted knowing that the Lord had been with us.

I ended the day and my time at IHOPKC at the Saturday night gathering praying for and hugging a beautiful young girl, as she cried and encountered Jesus's healing. She had seen her father killed and had to be adopted but was in a wonderful family. She kept thanking me for being like the grandma she had dreamt of having but never had! What a way to end my week, seeing restoration and a child experiencing family in the kingdom.

I flew back to Toronto to join Chris in time for the "Consumed Ladies Conference" at CTF. Once again, I had been so unaware of how Holy Spirit was leading me and drawing me into the Presence of the Lord. I was learning about encountering Jesus, the Bridegroom and experiencing the power of his love. According to Wiktionary, a definition of consumed is "to completely occupy the thoughts". In the Christian context Holy Spirit was inviting me to completely occupy my thoughts with the fire and passion of seeking God first.

Julie Meyer, worship leader and speaker on prayer and revival from IHOPKC, was one of our speakers! Julie is so in love with

Jesus, so full of passionate zeal and she started her talk by saying the definition of being successful "is knowing that we are loved by God".

"We love Him because He first loved us."

1 John 4:19

We are His passion, we are His excellence, and we are His good idea! Why is it that for too many of us it takes so long for us to fully realise how much we are loved by our Heavenly Father? Yet the Bible is full of God's love for His people. Julies' passion is to see the Bride being made ready for her Bridegroom, Jesus.

Let us rejoice and exalt him and give him glory, because the wedding celebration of the Lamb has come, and His bride has made herself ready (she loves him)

Revelation 19:7 (TPT)

Almost 10 years to the day since, I heard Suzanne in August 2023 pray these amazing words,

"A bride will not be radiant unless she knows she is loved. What the world sees right now in the church is a downtrodden unworthy bride who is not ready, so Lord we ask, will you cause your bride to be awakened with your love, overwhelmed by your love that she would arise radiant for all to see?

That she will be ready for your coming, walking with her head held high for those around to see that perfect love casts out all fear. That she would know that all power and all authority have been given to her in this realm. Clothe your bride in your love, clothe your bride in your strength, and clothe your bride in your power, that she may be undefeated and glorious."

Four weeks earlier, in 2013, I had seen a bride, Tania; radiant, knowing she was loved and walking down the aisle to marry our son Tim. At the service I read,

"Heaven's kingdom realm is also like a jewel merchant in search of rare pearls. When he discovered one very precious and exquisite pearl, he immediately gave up all he had in exchange for it."

Matthew 13:45-46. (TPT)

The notes in the Passion translation say Jesus is the merchant; we are the exquisite and unique pearl. He gave it all up; His life for us in exchange for having us as His very own!

We are His "one thing."

Chapter 14

Fire

"God is taking you to new levels of burning for Him, God is opening doors for you to be this fiery woman that sets ablaze places that are dry."

Prophecy 2013

We were in Canada for Thanksgiving in October 2013, and we celebrated by going to our favourite Hotel in Algonquin National Park. Holy Spirit was going to teach me about fire! My heart was crying out: "I want a burning heart for you Lord just like John the Baptist!"

"John was a blazing, shining torch..."

John 5:35 (TPT)

'God makes his Ministers a Flame of Fire'

Hebrews 1:7.

Around this time at KAN, we were singing,

"Set a fire down in my soul that I can't contain, that I can't control. I want more of you God, I want more of you."

Another song that came to mind that had impacted me in the 1990's about fire was,

"He has fire in His eyes and a sword in His hand and He's riding a white horse across this land and He's calling out to you and me, will you ride with me? We say yes, yes Lord, we will ride".

Holy Spirit was illuminating fire whenever anyone spoke or in any song that was sung. I heard Patricia King speaking about the refiner's fire from Malachi 3 and her exhortation was,

"Seek the fire, speak the fire, and you will endure the fire."

Prophet Bob Jones shared a dream about a house that was ablaze, and people were running to the fire. Police cordons, tape and roadblocks were not stopping them; they were so desperate to get to the fire! He believed that the house represented the church, and it was about to catch fire.

The glory of the Lord is going to fill the church in such an extraordinary way that it is going to be contagious. People will come from near and far to feel the presence and power of the Holy Spirit's baptism of fire. We needed it ten years ago, but we need it so much more now.

Back to Algonquin! The giants of the National Park are the White Pines, whose trunks are perfect for the masts of sailing vessels. The key to successful growth (according to the great booklet we picked up) is a forest fire.

"The fire had to be hot enough to burn off the dead leaves on the forest floor and expose the mineral soil needed for pine seedling germination and it had to be hot enough to kill off enough of the overhead trees to create the right conditions of sunlight for little pine trees down on the forest floor. Finally, the fire would have to occur just before the release of abundant white pine seeds from trees in or near the burnt area. If even one more than a year elapsed before pine seeds fell onto the burned area, other species might already have such a good head start that there would be no chance for the pines to catch up."

All the white pines we were seeing were approximately 220 years old, strongly suggesting that they all owe their origin to a forest fire of just the right strength back in the year 1790.

The booklet went on to point out one tree,

> **"The triangular scar at the base of this pine tree is a reminder of just how important fire is for white pines. Called church doors: when a ground fire is hot enough to kill the tree's living tissue under the protective bark, it produces a shape like a church door. The fire killed off the other competing trees enabling the white pine to put on a growth spurt."**

The other interesting fact is that white pine needles are in clusters of five, the number of grace and in the Hebrew language it can mean power, strength, prayer, fruitfulness, fast movement and anointed.

The analogy of what Holy Spirit fire does was amazing. Fire clears away the old: that which cannot normally be penetrated. The fire of the Holy Spirit burns away old wineskins to make way for the new.

Meshach, Shadrach and Abednego passionately believed that God would save them from the fire, but even if He did not, they put their trust in Him.

Fire prunes and clears away anything that gets in the way of the light coming through. Fire refines and purifies.

"I counsel you to buy from Me gold refined in the fire, that you may be rich."

Revelation 3:18

"...when you walk through the fire, you shall not be burned..."

Isaiah 43:2

"That the genuineness of your faith, being much more precious than gold that perishes, though it is tested by fire, may be found to praise, honour and glory at the revelation of Jesus Christ".

1 Peter 1:7

Back in CTF, two weeks later, five fire engines arrived in response to the fire alarms being tested! Someone said, "They were sent away without quenching the flames!"

A quote from Smith Wigglesworth from the book "The Baptism of Fire," says,

"Repeat in your heart often, baptized in the Holy Ghost and FIRE, FIRE, FIRE! All the unction and weeping, and travailing comes through the baptism of FIRE.

And I say to you, and I say to myself, purged and cleansed and filled with renewed spiritual power.

We must with our whole hearts believe the baptism of the Holy Ghost is meant to make us FLAMES of FIRE. John the Baptist said concerning Jesus, 'He shall BAPTIZE you with the Holy Ghost and with FIRE.' God's ministers are to be a FLAME of FIRE - a perpetual flame; a constant fire; a continual burning flame, burning and shining lights. God has nothing less for us than to be FLAMES of FIRE. We must have a living faith in God, a faith that God's great might and power may burn in us until our whole life is energised by the power of God.

I see people from time to time very slack, cold, and indifferent, but after they get filled with the Holy Spirit, they become ablaze for God. I believe God's ministers are to be FLAMES of FIRE: nothing less than FLAMES; nothing less than mighty instruments with BURNING messages. I say all these things to you to move you into a living faith in God. God wants to flow through you with measureless power of divine utterance and grace until your whole body is a FLAME of FIRE. God intends each soul in Pentecost to be a live wire. Not a monument but a movement.

If you want to increase in the life of God, then you must settle it in your heart that you will not at any time resist the Holy Spirit. The Holy Ghost and FIRE - the FIRE BURNING up everything that would impoverish and destroy you. If you are not on FIRE, you are not in the place where God can mightily use you. It is only the FIRE of God that BURNS up the entanglements of the world.

My prayer is for us to hear the alarm being sounded. To wake up: to be made ready and cry out for the FIRE to come. Holy Spirit, come. Cleanse us, purify us, renew us, and fill us with passion for Jesus! Stir us up to cry out for more of the FIRE.

BAPTISE us with your FIRE Holy Spirit!

Chapter 15

Preparation of the Bride

My journals record several dreams from 2012-2014 about weddings!

My hat went missing and I could not find it and in another I was part of the Bridal party but we were not ready!

When I asked the Lord what these were all about, I sensed that I represented the church and the busyness that so easily distracts us from being ready for our Bridegroom Jesus. Holy Spirit said,

"It is the Lord's call to us all at this time to lead the way as we demonstrate to the church God's agenda is as we draw closer to Jesus' return."

"You will play an integral part in the preparation of my Bride, to receive her king. The Lord says I am preparing worshipping warriors to call forth my church into position for I am coming quicker than you think."

"Then the Kingdom of heaven shall be likened to ten virgins who took their lamps and went out to meet the bridegroom. Now five of them were wise and five were foolish. Those who were foolish took their lamps and took no oil with them, but the wise took oil in their vessels with their lamps. But while the bridegroom was delayed they all slumbered and slept.

At midnight a cry was heard: behold the bridegroom is coming; go out to meet Him! Then all those virgins arose and trimmed their lamps. And the foolish said to the wise, give us some of your oil, for our lamps are going out. But the wise answered, saying, no lest there should not be enough for us and you; but go rather to those who sell, and buy for yourselves. And while they went to buy, the bridegroom came, and those who were ready went in with Him to the wedding; and the door was shut.

Matthew 25:1-13

To be the Bride we need to be intimate with our Bridegroom! It's the oil of intimacy; intimacy produces oil to keep our lamps burning.

Many will remember the old song,

> **"Give me oil in my lamp, keep me burning, give me oil in my lamp I pray, give me oil in my lamp keep me burning, keep me burning 'til the break of day."**

I've just heard an interesting fact about olive oil: the purer the olive oil is, the more easily it catches fire! The purer our hearts are for Jesus the more easily we will be set on fire for Him. We will become those burning ones set on fire to set others on fire!

Holy Spirit has been drawing me to Jesus to know Him more intimately and as I have responded His promise is that He will burn away everything that hinders that intimacy.

I have been blessed to be part of Kingdom Advance Network (KAN), whose objective is,

> **"Preparing and mobilising believers to extend the Kingdom in anticipation of the return of Jesus."**

Let us be glad and rejoice and give Him glory, for the marriage of the Lamb has come, and His wife has made herself ready. And to her it was granted to be arrayed in fine linen, clean and bright, for the fine linen is the righteous acts of the saints.

Revelation 19:7-9 NKJV

As if to reinforce this message of getting ready for Jesus' return, I was given two copies of "Jesus Calling", a daily devotional written by Sarah Young, as a birthday gift in 2018. One came from Sue and the other from my sister-in-law Irene. Both had been prompted by Holy Spirit to give them to me. Sue had written, "I pray you will experience His presence more deeply as you embark on each new day lived for Jesus."

I had not used a daily devotional for many years but Holy Spirit has a wonderful sense of humour and knew that I needed the discipline of following one, and had to trust that Holy Spirit knew better than me what I needed.

"Trust in the Lord completely, and do not rely on your own opinions, with all your heart rely on Him to guide you, and He will lead you in every decision you make. Become intimate with Him in whatever you do, and He will lead you wherever you go. Don't think for a moment that you know it all, for wisdom comes when you adore Him with undivided devotion."

Proverbs 3:5-7 TPT

Holy Spirit keeps reminding me of this scripture! And I chuckle at how many opinions I have. But I love the Lord and Paul says,

"I pray with great faith for you because I am fully convinced that the One who began this glorious work in you will faithfully continue the process of maturing you and will put His finishing touches to it until the unveiling of our Lord Jesus Christ."

Philippians 1:6 TPT

Oh, thank you Lord, we are a work in progress! And You are preparing us as the Bride to be pure and spotless, ready for Jesus' return.

Chapter 16

Prayer

In 2003, Jenny (Apostolic Leader at KAN) started to mentor me and a small group of ladies from Prayer School, each of us were given a short talk to prepare and mine was "Abiding". I remember struggling to know what to say as I had no real understanding of the word!

Fast forward to twenty years later and now when I think of abiding there is such a deep longing inside of me for more of Jesus.

Abide in me and I in you. As the branch cannot bear fruit of itself, unless it abides in the vine, neither can you, unless you abide in Me. I am the vine, you are the branches. He who abides in Me and I in him, bears much fruit; but without Me you can do nothing.

John 15:4-5

This is part of the journey I've been on! For me to learn how to abide!

"He who ***dwells*** *in the secret place of the Most High shall abide under the shadow of the Almighty."*

Psalm 91:1.

My memories take me back to a fiction book called "Mister God, This is Anna" which I read in the late 70s. Anna, the central character, was a four year old child full of innocence and wisdom but who also had an intimate relationship with Mister God. She talked about a God shaped hole inside of us! I remember not being able to understand the book but it both intrigued and frustrated me! But I know that around this time my hunger for God started.

Prayer connected the dots; even before I gave my life to Jesus at the Billy Graham Mission, I had started to pray as part of a prayer triplet.

Prayer played a major part of my life at St Editha's. A small group of us met weekly at the local Town Hall to pray for transformation. If there was a call to pray, I was there!

My natural desire to pray was further fuelled during my visit to India, when Holy Spirit further ignited my prayer life. This set me up for KAN and Prayer School in Burton on Trent.

I had found amazing, passionate, fiery, excited people (mainly women) who loved praying as much as me! We were and still are a company of Worshipping Prayer Warriors.

We were trained "on the job": as I mentioned early, I took part in strategic prayer assignments in Rome; Naples; Berlin; Luxemburg and Brussels. As well as visiting nearly every county town in England for a worship, prayer and Prophetic event.

I have been on at least five visits to Israel to pray and to see the sites and then, because I love it, to take others as part of a tour.

As I look back I see Holy Spirit was wooing and drawing me into a deeper relationship with Jesus, step by step, prayer by prayer!

Prayer often is fuelled by our needs; the church is flourishing throughout the world where there is much persecution.

"My fellow believers, when it seems as though you are facing nothing but difficulties see it an invaluable opportunity to experience the greatest joy that you can! For I know that when your faith is tested, it stirs up power within you to endure all things. And then as your endurance grows even stronger it will release perfection into every part of your being until there is nothing missing and nothing lacking."

James 1:2-4.TPT.

Prayer fills the pages of this book and yet I never wanted to be labelled as an intercessor, because of the picture that conjured up in my head. Beni Johnson had similar thoughts as I read in her book the "Happy Intercessor."

"I grew up in a church where the intercessors did not look like happy people a lot of the time. From my small perspective, all those who were intercessors were the ones who walked around with what looked to me like very heavy burdens. The intercessors always looked sad to me; I don't remember seeing them smile."

My prayer life has been far from that because Holy Spirit has led me and continues to lead me into the most amazing adventures in prayer; whether it is prayer for my family, healing prayer, warfare prayer, decrees or declaration prayer.

During the last few years, we've been given a platform to use Zoom for prayer; we can now pray with anyone anywhere! The pandemic gave me the opportunity to pray as part of an online Healing Room with people from all over the world. How amazing and creative is our God!

1 Thessalonians 5:17 says, *"Pray without ceasing"*. This implies that continuous prayer is a lifestyle, or as the Passion translation says *"Make your life a prayer"* which is the surrender of ourselves to God and His ways.

I have seen many answers to prayer in my life many of which I have already written about earlier in this book, but a few stand out and even now cause me to marvel at our amazing God.

In 1999 our youngest son was in his final year at a fee paying private school when Chris was made redundant, and we had no idea where each terms fees were coming from, but step by step we saw God provide.

Our house mortgage was with a Building Society, who decided to change to a Bank at this very time and had issued shares to everyone who had money invested or had a mortgage. The timing was perfect; our shares when sold paid one term's fees! Then we looked at what we had that we could sell. We had some very old hand painted magic lantern slides that had come from Chris's Aunts' house, so off they went to auction. On the day of the auction Chris was at work so I was there alone, the sale room was buzzing and I was excited but not prepared for what was about to happen! The slides were divided into four lots and as each lot sold the price got higher, in the end I could hardly believe that we had raised three times more money than expected and another term of fees were paid! Gods timing is always perfect and ever since then I have occasionally, just out of interest, checked on the value of Magic Lantern slides and they have never reached the prices of that amazing auction day!

"**Man pulled alive from an avalanche**" is my journal entry for January 3, 2005, as we skied with friends in the French Alps.

We heard about the avalanche that had just happened because our friend Peter was chatting on the ski lift to a man who was going to look for his friend who he believed had been caught up in an avalanche.

We stopped to have lunch and a helicopter came down near us and parked by the ski chair lift. One hour later, we were on the chair lift going up the mountain, passing the still stationary helicopter and I suddenly started to decree and declare that it was not too late for the man to be found alive. My faith began to increase, and I continued to pray and suddenly we heard the helicopter take off and land near the area of the avalanche, where we could see a stretcher being lifted up and put into the helicopter. I knew immediately that a miracle had taken place and I had been in the right place at the right time to pray.

It was confirmed later by a random man in the ski queue, who turned to me and said, “Be careful of avalanches”. He then said, “It was a miracle”!

I know that Holy Spirit stirred me to decree and declare life and then things started to happen. We later found out that the man found alive was buried for an hour under three metres of snow before he had been found! How many opportunities do we all miss to pray and believe for the impossible?

Chapter 17

Restoration

I grew up in the 50s and 60s in a loving home with a father and grandfather who were freemasons. Many years later I asked my father why he had joined the freemasons and his reply was to find Jesus! He hadn't.

I was to discover that Freemasonry is an occult organization full of secret oaths that teaches that,

"Jesus was just a man, one of the great men of the past but not divine and not the son of God".

The Mason is faced with the choice of whom he will serve: Jesus the saviour of his soul, or the tolerant god of Freemasonry who leads him to destruction!

I gained a revelation of how this worked at a Christian retreat I attended in the late 90s. We were asked to put together a collage of cuttings from magazines that depicted our family life growing up as a child. As I put together my picture it was full of colour, it was vibrant and exciting but then I suddenly started to stick grey fabric and cotton wool on top and sensed Holy Spirit say, "this is what freemasonry did to your family, it covered you all in greyness and tried to take all the joy!" Prior to this if anyone had asked if I had a happy childhood, I would have said yes but it held no excitement! So it was a light bulb moment! Jesus had unveiled and restored the joy of my early family life to me.

"And He will send you Jesus the Messiah, the chosen One for you. For He must remain in heaven, until the restoration of all things has taken place, fulfilling everything that God said long ago through His holy prophets".

Acts 3:20-21 (TPT)

Restoration had been a part of my own young family's life with Chris and our boys in a quite concrete way. (No pun intended as Chris is a specialist in precast concrete!)

In 1981 we realised that we were outgrowing our little cottage which had given us three incredible years of joy. Our first child Ben had arrived, I had joined the church choir and we had formed some lifelong friendships, but we needed more space and were ready to move.

We found our next home, just a few miles away and it was a wreck! But Chris had the vision to see that this fifteenth century house could become the home of our dreams, where we could bring up our family.

The restoration process of our house began. It took 10 years to finish, and the first six months were spent living with an eighteen-month-old child in a sixteen-foot caravan! Decades later we are still living in the home of our dreams.

"So I will restore to you the years that the swarming locust has eaten, the crawling locust, the consuming locust and the chewing locust, My great army which I sent among you. You shall eat in plenty and be satisfied, and praise the name of the Lord your God, who has dealt wondrously with you and My people will never be put to shame"

Joel 2:25-26

Jesus reminds us in Acts 3:21 that He will restore all things when He returns!

God sent His son to die for us, to bring us back into His family and provide a home!

Rachel Hickson, Director of Heartcry UK recently speaking at KAN said,

> **"Restoration goes back to original design, it takes time, it takes money, it takes patience, and restoration removes the covering, layer by layer and dismantles before reconstructing.**

"They will restore ruins from long ago and rebuild what was long devastated. They will renew ruined cities and desolations of past generations"

Isaiah 61:4 (TPT)

The notes in the passion translation read as follows:

"These desolate places can also point to areas of our lives that are broken and to spiritual truths that have been lost and forgotten for generations, which are now being recovered".

Isaiah 61:4

I find myself singing Lara Martin's song "Divine Exchange" as I write this,

"My heart is captivated Lord, by You alone,
Captured by the awesomeness of You alone, melted by the grace and mercy You have shown,
I stand in wonder.
I reach to You the One who made the blind eyes see, who breaks the chains of sickness with authority.
Restoring what was broken, so it may fly again.
I live to worship You, I breathe to worship You, all of my days Your face I will seek.
And as I worship You, You lead me to that place, to that place of divine exchange."

I am constantly amazed at how my loving heavenly Father reveals these truths through the Bible.

In the Hebrew, the verb meaning to build, and the word translated "son" come from the same root. Build is BANAH and son is BEN.

"Wisdom has built her house..."
Proverbs 9:1

The notes in the Passion translation say, "the house wisdom is building is a son." You and I are sons of God who are being built into a spiritual house.

"Banah" is #1129 in Strong's Concordance and it means "to erect, repair, and obtain children". We were restoring and rebuilding our house and our first sons' name was Ben!

The house wisdom is building is a son/heir and ultimately a family! God set the model. He came as a man to die for us, to bring us back into His family and provide a home!

"Having been built on the foundation of the apostles and prophets, Jesus Christ Himself being the chief cornerstone, in whom the whole building, being fitted together, grows into a holy temple in the Lord, in whom you also are being built together for a dwelling place of God in the Spirit."

Ephesians 2:20-22.

Jesus said to His disciples,

"In my Father's house there are many dwelling places (Homes). If it were not so, I would have told you: for I am going away to prepare a place for you".

John 14:2 (Amplified Bible)

As I write this now, I am reminded that as I have travelled and met many believers, it has been easy to connect because we are all part of a family, God's Kingdom family. We all have the DNA our heavenly Father, which also binds us together.

Jesus' prayer,

"I pray for them all to be joined together as one, even as you and I Father, are joined together as one. I pray for them to become one with us. So that the world will recognise that you sent me"

John 17:21 (TPT)

In September 2023 we entered 5784, Pey Dalit, the Hebraic year of the door. Since the beginning of time God has wanted a home and a family.

Steve (Apostolic leader at KAN) preaching on Sunday 29th September 2023 said,

"You and I are sons of God, He is building us into a spiritual house, we build the family name as we represent our heavenly Father on the earth".

Jane Smith who also preached at KAN in September 2023, said

"The door God opens will require you to depend on Him."

I heard Chuck Pierce, from Glory of Zion in Texas, USA say,

"The ERA (we are in) is about the voice that comes out of your house".

I believe this book is the manifestation of those prophetic words in my life. God has opened the door for my voice to be released in this way and I have had to depend on Him to do it! Bringing my old journal entries from the last 40 years has been somewhat of a restoration process as my adventures with God find a new home.

Thank You Holy Spirit for opening the door, many times in my life and I look forward to more adventures with you.

Would love to stay in touch:

Email: joyfuladventureswithgod@gmail.com
Follow me on
Instagram @jeanisfullofjoy

Notes

Cover

Mark Batterson "Wild goose Chase: Reclaim the adventure of pursuing God" (Multnomah books 2008)

Introduction

John Stanko gave me the prophetic word in 2009 at KAN Burton

Chapter 1,

My History is His Story Through Me

"Majesty" Jack Hayford. (Kevin Mayhew Ltd)

March for Jesus www.themarchforjesus.org

Chapter 2,

Time to Get Ready

Revival magazine article "Looking Back" John Arnott Senior Leader at TAC

Randy Shankle "The Merismos" page 230 (Whitaker House 1987)

Chapter 5,

Portland and Israel

Tommy Tenney "God Chasers" (Destiny Image 1999)

Chapter 7,

The Pearl of Great Price

"The Pearl of Great Price" vineyardchurches.org.uk

Chapter 8,

Girls Together

Stasi Eldredge "Captivating" (Nelson Books 2005)

Talk "She is no ordinary girl" Bobby Houston at Colour Conference, Hillsong 2004

Chapter 10,

Going to the Nations

Michael Kimuli "Effective Fervent Prayer" (New Wine Press 2002)

Chapter 11,

Canada

"Studies in the Song of Solomon: Progression of Holy Passion" (2007) Forerunner School of Ministry. www.IHOP.org

Duncan Smith "Consumed by Love" (Catch the Fire Books 2014)

Charles and Frances Hunter "Healing Prayers" (Whitaker House 2001)

Chapter 12,

Outreach and Evangelism

Kevin Dedmon "The Ultimate Treasure Hunt: A Guide to Supernatural Evangelism through Supernatural Encounters" (Destiny Image 2007)

Joshua Giles "Prophetic Forecast" (Chosen, Baker Publishing Group 2022)

Chapter 13,

IHOP, Kansas City

"Waymaker" song by Leeland (Album "Better Word")

Corey Stark "Ignite the Nations" www.IgniteTheNations111.org

Wiktionary www.wiktionary.org

Julie Meyer www.juliemeyerministries.com

Chapter 14,

Fire

"Set a Fire" Will Reagan & United Pursuit Band (Album "Live At The Banks House" 2010)

"We will Ride" Linedell Cooley (Album "Revival at Brownsville" 1995)

Dr. Michael H Yeager "Smith Wigglesworth; The Baptism of Fire" (Independently Published 2023)

Chapter 15,

Preparing the Bride

Sarah Young "Jesus Calling" (Thomas Nelson 2004)

Chapter 16,

Prayer

Fynn "Mr God, This is Anna" (Harper Collins Publishers 1977)

Beni Johnson "The Happy Intercessor" (Destiny Image 2009)

Chapter 17,

Restoration

Talk by Rachel Hickson Director of Heartcry UK

Lara Martin "Divine Exchange" (Album "Your Love Never Fails"

Mission Worship 2010)

Printed in Great Britain
by Amazon

45568057R00096